MIDI
The Ins, Outs & Thrus
by Jeff Rona

Edited by RONNY S. SCHIFF
Associate Editor SCOTT R. WILKINSON
Graphic Design & Illustrations by ELYSE MORRIS WYMAN
Diagrams by ALBERT DUGAS & JEFFREY C. RONA
Computer Cover Graphics by COLIN CANTWELL

MIDI
The Ins, Outs & Thrus

by Jeff Rona

Library of Congress Cataloging-in-Publication Data

Rona, Jeffrey C. (Jeffrey Carl), 1957-
MIDI, the ins, outs & thrus.

1. MIDI (Standard)   2. Computer sound processing.
I. Schiff, Ronny.   II. Title.   III. Title: MIDI, the ins,
outs, and thrus.
MT723.R66   1987   789.9'9   86-27746
ISBN 0-88188-560-6

HAL LEONARD BOOKS

8112 W. Bluemound Road
Milwaukee, Wisconsin 53213

Table of Contents

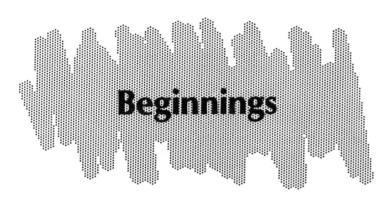

Chapter 1

Beginnings

The way music is made has been changed forever. MIDI instruments are now the tools of artists from an enormous range of styles and traditions. The quality, and perhaps even the quantity of music has grown as a result of the MIDI phenomenon.

The 'sixties and 'seventies were an explosive time for the creation of new musical instruments. The monophonic Moog and ARP synthesizers were already bending quite a few ears by the late 'seventies when Oberheim introduced the first polyphonic synthesizer. It was a four-voice analog keyboard with an array of knobs and switches; it produced some especially good brass and bass sounds.

Then more and more polyphonic synthesizers began to appear: Sequential Circuits, Yamaha, Moog, Roland, ARP and other companies introduced new models of synthesizers, all able to play multiple notes simultaneously.

After polyphony, perhaps the next most important advance in synthesizer technology was the incorporation of programmable memory into instruments. Since a polyphonic synthesizer must have some sort of built-in computer to "look" at the keyboard and assign keys to oscillators (the actual tone making circuitry), that small computer could also help store and recall sounds created by the user, and not just factory presets. This opened up a whole new world for live performance. Prior to programmable memory, the reason that people like Keith Emerson and Rick Wakeman had such extravagant keyboard setups on stage was that each of the instruments could only be set-up to produce a single sound per show. Hours of preparation were needed to patch together the sounds and the different instruments. When memory came along, it allowed a single synthesizer to be used for different sounds during a live show or session.

Figure 1-1

Keith Emerson's photo by Will Alexander

Adding memory to the synthesizer made it many times more useful. But synthesizers — like some cars — have personalities of their own. Some get wonderful, thick brass. Others may be more adept at woodwinds, or strings, or bells, or sound effects, or pianos, or colorful tropical birds, or the laugh of small friendly aliens. What was needed next was a way to combine the best of each instrument into a musical system.

So, a technique that some players adopted to create new sounds was to play the same part on two keyboards at the same time, one hand on each instrument. A keyboardist could then use each instrument to its best advantage: strings from the "string synth," brass from the "brass synth," and so on. This was an awkward technique at best, and one's polyphony was limited to the number of fingers on one hand, typically five.

Joe Zawinul of Weather Report developed a technique for playing on two keyboards simultaneously. He placed himself between a pair of ARP 2600s, one of which had its keyboard electronically reversed, going from high notes on the left to low on the right:

All these measures were designed to accomplish one thing — getting the most from these great new instruments. The layering of sounds upon sounds became an important tool, almost like a trademark sound for some of these and other artists.

Then came the next big step: Some new keyboards were coming equipped with computer interfaces built into them. Instruments from both Oberheim (the OBX) and Rhodes (the Chroma) could, for the first time, be connected to another of the same model of synthesizer. This was an improvement since sounds could be layered on top of each other, but didn't answer the big question of how to connect *different* instruments together for unique combinations.

Figure 1-2 Joe Zawinul

One person who took matters into his own hands was Herbie Hancock. Newly enthralled with the technology of synthesizers, he spent a small fortune to have many of his instruments custom modified to be interfaceable with each other. For the first time, instruments of different makes were connected together by means of a common, though custom, analog/digital connection.

Figure 1-3

Figure 1-4

By this time, more and more musicians were approaching the instrument makers to try and get their own equipment to interconnect. In addition, the first digital *sequencers* (a device that records the performance played on an instrument and can then play it back) were starting to show up. These sequencers, such as the Roland Micro-Composer and the Oberheim DSX, were yet another reason to want compatibility between products from the different instrument makers. The Roland Micro — Composer was a four-track sequencer that produced either control voltages for earlier synthesizers or used a special "Roland only" digital connector. Oberheim's sequencer was quite a bit more sophisticated, but was limited to use only with the company's OB synthesizers.

Time For A Change

Time was ripe for a change to occur in the music industry by the early 'eighties. Synthesizers were no longer a *techno-oddity,* and sales of instruments to the mass market, as well as to professionals, were growing quickly. There were more companies involved as well. The diversity of keyboards, drum machines, sequencers, and such, was growing rapidly. To move up another notch in technology, the synthesizer industry needed to take a lesson from the computer industry.

The computer industry has for many years depended upon certain standards to ensure compatibility between computers and other devices. For example, the *modem* is a device that lets computers exchange information by telephone. It makes no difference what the makes, models or cost of the computers are, they can connect and exchange information. Other examples of computer industry standards are floppy disks (only two or three major formats), printers, cables, disk drives, memory chips, and many types of software. Compatibility strengthened the new personal computer industry and was a major factor in its amazing success.

Twice a year the members of the National Association of Music Merchants (NAMM) meet to show new musical products and find new ways to market musical instruments and accessories. During one of these conventions in 1982, a meeting of a small group of synthesizer manufacturers took place at the request of Dave Smith, President of Sequential Circuits. Engineers from many of the major companies were in attendance. They discussed a proposal for the adoption of a *standard for the transmitting and receiving of musical performance information digitally between all types of electronic musical instruments.* The original proposal was called UMI, for Universal Musical Interface.

The original proposal went through a significant number of revisions before becoming the *Musical Instrument Digital Interface,* or MIDI standard. Several large Japanese instrument companies became involved in engineering the final version. In 1983, Sequential Circuits and Roland introduced the first MIDI keyboards. Since its introduction, MIDI has continued to grow and improve. New ideas have been added or more clearly defined. A great deal of room was left for expansion without sacrificing the main power of MIDI-compatibility with all existing MIDI instruments.

This book is a guide for the musician, performer, producer, composer, engineer, computer enthusiast, student, or anyone wanting to get a good understanding of how MIDI works, and how to work with MIDI. It will assist you in learning the nuts and bolts of MIDI technology. The more you understand how MIDI operates, the easier it is to use the musical tools it provides. You will develop an understanding of how a MIDI system for any occasion can be put together quickly and easily.

You will gain the knowledge needed to make sound (pun intended) purchases of MIDI and MIDI-related equipment. You will learn how to get the most out of any musical situation that calls for using MIDI. Examples of many different MIDI systems are shown to help with the creation of the right music system for your needs and budget. You will probably be surprised at just how simple MIDI is to understand and use. As your knowledge about MIDI increases, you will see the wonderful possibilities available to you from the technology of music.

1979 — Synthesizer engineers see the need for MIDI.

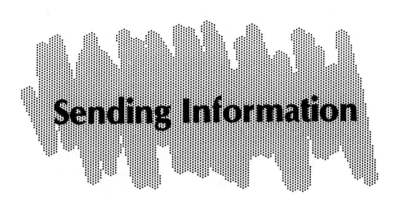

Chapter 2

Sending Information

Telephones and cable television use electricity to send information over wires. MIDI does exactly that, though in a slightly different way. MIDI uses the same technology that computers do to relay information.

Figure 2-1

When you speak on the telephone, the microphone in your phone's handset converts the sound of your voice into electricity. The speaker on the telephone to which you are connected converts that electricity back into sound. A second wire sends sound from the other phone back to yours. This is a simple circuit, *but its simplicity makes it no less powerful!*

Storing Information

Computers are also able to communicate to each other over wires, but they do so rather differently. To understand this difference, take a brief look at the inside of one:

Figure 2-2

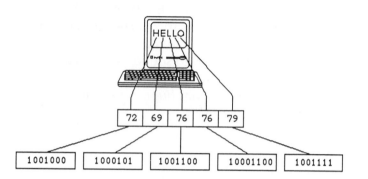

The next question to be answered is: How does a machine store a number? The answer is that small bits of electricity, appropriately called "bits," in the memory of the computer store patterns that represent the values of the numbers. Those bits of electricity are represented on paper as "1s" or "0s." This stems from the earliest computers, which used actual switches to represent numbers. Since a switch can only be either on or off, the same is true for a "bit" of information.

A computer, then, can communicate with other computers simply by sending these bits over a wire. A receiving computer will store the bits in its own memory to re-form the information. For any other computer to receive and understand this information, some standard way of sending it must be used, just as telephones all use the same kind of wiring, dialing system, microphones, and speakers.

As seen in the example above, it can take quite a few 1s and 0s to say something. It took forty bits just to say "HELLO." Some computer systems can send information over a wire several bits at a time. This technique is called *parallel transmission* and it looks something like this:

Figure 2-3

The picture above shows the screen of a friendly computer with the word *HELLO* on it. No matter how a computer may show information to a person — either words on a screen, lights on a synthesizer front panel, or the sounds stored in the instrument — it can only represent that information internally as *numbers in its memory* (more on this later). Below the computer are the numbers that most computers use to store the letters for the word "HELLO." Each letter is represented by a code number inside the computer. Computers use numbers to store all information inside them.

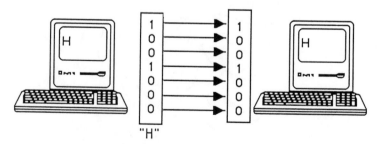

There is another technique for sending information from computer to computer. Instead of sending several bits of information simultaneously over several wires, the bits leave the computer in a single file line over a single wire:

Figure 2-4

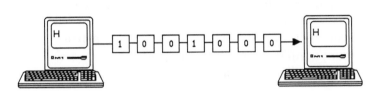

At the other end of the line, the receiver picks up the bits and reassembles them. This is called *serial transmission* since the bits are moving serially (one after another) through the wire.

Nearly all computers today use one of these two methods of communication — serial or parallel. There are advantages and drawbacks to each. Parallel is generally faster, but the hardware and cables can be expensive. Parallel cables can also behave like very good antennae, sending and receiving interference, and cannot be longer than a few feet. Serial communication, on the other hand, while a bit slower, does not cost nearly as much, and the cables can be very long — fifty feet or more.

Sending MIDI

Knowing this information, the creators of MIDI had to decide which kind of transmission to utilize, serial or parallel. The disadvantages of parallel well outweighed its advantages, and so they chose serial. Let's see that in big letters:

MIDI USES SERIAL TRANSMISSION

Parallel transmission was found to be too expensive for use in low-priced instruments. More importantly, it would also limit the distance over which MIDI could be transmitted to just a few feet,

making it very impractical for on-stage use. As mentioned above, parallel cables can create strong interference that might cause humming or other noise in audio systems. Stage lighting systems and powerful amplifiers can also have a negative effect on a parallel cable by garbling some of the information as it passes through the cable. This in turn could have a catastrophic effect on the synthesizer playing the data, which could also have a bad effect on your ability to get more work as a musician.

Serial data transmission was the logical choice for use with musical instruments. To keep it simple and inexpensive (so everyone could get their hands on it), the creators of MIDI chose a simple five pin plug called a *DIN plug.* It had been used for many applications before in audio and video, but not much involving electronic musical instruments. Thus it would not be confused with other connectors such as audio or AC. The DIN connector looks like this:

Figure 2-5 A MIDI 5 Pin DIN Plug

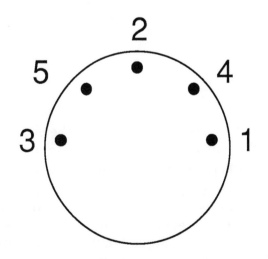

Serial data transmission needs only a single wire to send information from machine to machine, as was mentioned above. What are the functions of the other four wires?

Figure 2-6

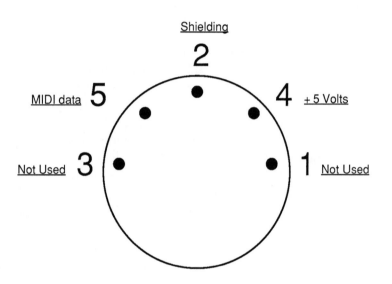

Since MIDI uses only a single wire in the cable to send information, the information travels in only one direction over a single MIDI cable. The MIDI system had to be devised to allow information to go in both directions. At the same time, MIDI had to be able to pass data on to a third, fourth, or fifth instrument (or as many synthesizers as you can afford). To accomplish this, it was decided to have three separate connectors on each MIDI instrument: one to send the data out, one to receive data in, and one more to pass incoming data on through *(thru)* to another MIDI instrument. Here is what a typical MIDI instrument's MIDI connectors (or "ports" as they are usually called) look like:

Figure 2-7

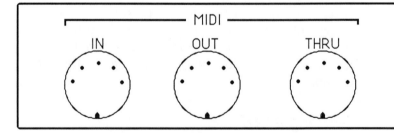

Not all the pins (the connectors at the end of the cable) are used:

• **Pin 1** and **Pin 3** are not used at all.

• **Pin 2** is used as shielding. That means it is attached to a wire that wraps around all the other wires in the cable. This helps prevent it from sending and receiving any interference that might ruin the data in the cable.

• **Pin 4** is a 5-volt current loop to ensure that electricty flows in the proper direction.

• **Pin 5** is the real sender of MIDI!!

These three connectors — IN, OUT, and THRU — are found on nearly all MIDI devices. There will be exceptions from time to time, as you'll see later on; but this is what is found on the vast majority of MIDI instruments.

MIDI OUT

MIDI does not send sound over wires like audio components in a stereo system. It sends digital codes that *represent* what is being played on the instrument. As someone plays on a MIDI keyboard, his or her *performance* is examined by a computer in the instrument. The musician's actions are translated into the MIDI code and the information is sent out through the MIDI OUT port.

MIDI IN

The MIDI IN connector receives any incoming MIDI information and treats it as though it were an action being performed *on* the instrument itself. Polyphonic synthesizers, drum machines, and sequencers all depend on built-in microcomputer chips to perform their various functions. They are, in the current parlance, "intelligent." In a keyboard synthesizer, for example, there is a small computer circuit whose job it is to constantly watch the keyboard and detect any time a key is pressed or released. It sends this information on to the rest of the synthesizer for the creation of the sound itself. Similarly, a computer within a synthesizer will watch the MIDI IN port and send the proper commands to the rest of the synthesizer to create sounds.

MIDI THRU

In order to be able to send MIDI data on to other synthesizers, a MIDI port called THRU duplicates anything that comes to MIDI IN. It is a "repeater." An important idea to remember is that *anything played on a keyboard only goes out the MIDI OUT, and not the MIDI THRU.*

Figure 2-8

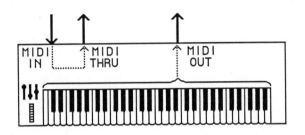

These three connectors — IN, OUT, and THRU — are the complete backbone of MIDI hardware. Understanding these will give you the basis for being able to put together even the most complex MIDI system. Examples will be shown throughout the book to further illustrate the functions of these three MIDI ports.

MIDI data moves in a single direction through the cable (as seen through a high power microscope).

Chapter 3

What MIDI Sends — A Musical Breakdown

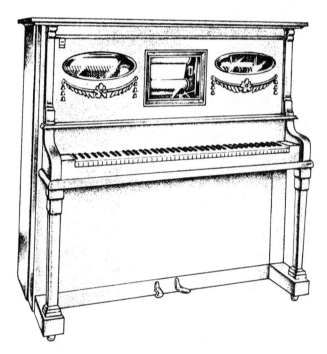

The old player piano — a marvel of technology in its time: A roll of paper with holes in it passes over a metal bar. There are holes in the metal bar for each key of the piano. A vacuum pump inside the piano draws air in through the bar. When a hole in the paper comes over a hole in the bar, air is drawn in and triggers a mechanism to move the hammer onto the appropriate string and strike the note. There was a special recording piano built solely for creating the paper rolls. The player pianos that people bought were for playback only, not unlike a record player. As far as dynamics or nuance were concerned, they didn't exist on the player piano. Each key was struck with exactly the same force, creating a performance that might at best be called forceful, and at worst cacophonous.

With the player piano, what was "encoded" on the paper wasn't the actual sound of a piano, but simply what was *played* on the piano. The main idea behind MIDI is quite similar: to allow what is performed on one instrument to be played by any other instrument, or to record that performance and play it again later. MIDI has the added benefit of being able to record and play back a performance *simultaneously*. While someone plays a MIDI keyboard, any number of additional MIDI instruments can be following the performance and playing right along. It would be just as if the player were sitting at every one of the instruments and playing them all at once.

While MIDI is used for a wide range of instruments, such as drums and guitars, its design is based on the keyboard. There is a small computer in any MIDI keyboard that senses when a key is pressed or when it is released and immediately converts these actions into MIDI information in the form of a computer code.

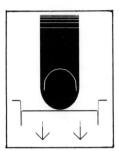

Pressing A Key

• When a key is pressed on a MIDI keyboard, a command is sent out which says "a key has just been pressed!" That short message is followed by two more: The first says *which* key was pressed: middle C, or A flat below middle C, etc. The second one indicates *how quickly* a key has been pressed, which will tell other instruments about the dynamics of the note just played.

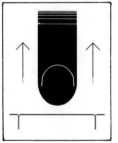

Releasing A Key

• MIDI treats the pressing of a key and the releasing of a key as two completely different actions. MIDI doesn't look at music in terms of the length of time that notes are held, because an instrument doesn't wait until the note is finished before sending out information about it. The moment a key is pressed the code indicating that is sent, and the moment it is released then *another* code is sent.

Wheels And Pedals

Typical MIDI instruments have one or more knobs, wheels, pedals, or levers to control various expressive parameters such as *pitch bending, modulation,* and *sustain.* In MIDI these are called *Continuous Controllers,* and each of these has its own special code:

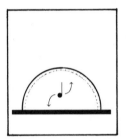

• There is a MIDI code for the *pitch bend wheel.* Moving it either up or down will produce a code. The code does not say what the pitch is, nor how far the pitch is bent. It simply represents the current position of the wheel.

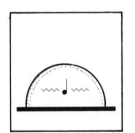

• Most keyboards have a *modulation wheel* or *lever* for adding vibrato to a sound. MIDI has a code for the movement of the wheel; the farther the wheel is turned, the larger the value of the code and the more intense the vibrato.

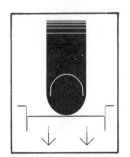

• Many MIDI keyboards can sense if pressure is applied to a key after it has been struck. This is called *aftertouch,* and is used for effects such as vibrato or brightness. MIDI has two different codes for aftertouch: One sends a value for the entire keyboard. The second one can send an individual value for each key. Because of the expense of putting an aftertouch sensor under each key, this second code is rarely used.

Programs

• Nearly all MIDI devices have some sort of memory. Synthesizers remember sounds, drum machines remember rhythmic patterns, and effects processors remember parameter settings. These sets of stored information are called *programs.* There is a code in MIDI called *Program Change* that tells an instrument to change to a specific memory number.

Switches

• Like pianos, most synthesizers use pedals for sustaining notes played on the keyboard

and for other functions. Some of the Continuous Controllers in MIDI are used specifically for pedals and switches. Like the keys on a keyboard, a code is sent when the pedal is pressed, and another is sent when it is released. Other Continuous Controllers are used for setting overall volume, balance, breath control, panning controls, and controlling the depth of external effects such as tremolo, chorus, or phasing.

Synchronizing

• There is a wide range of MIDI instruments that have clocks in them. Sequencers and drum machines can be linked and synchronized automatically by a part of MIDI called *System Real Time.* Real Time messages let one instrument tell others how fast to play, when to start, when to stop, when to change tempo, where to begin within a piece, and even which song to play.

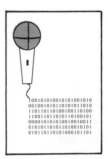

Sample Dumps

• *Samplers* (instruments that record acoustic sounds into digital memory and then play them back) use large amounts of memory to store sounds. A way is needed to allow these instruments to transmit all that information to and from computers and other sampling instruments. MIDI has brought these instruments closer together, too. The *Sample Dump Standard* is a code that lets different samplers exchange sounds and send their sounds to computers.

MIDI breaks a musical performance into many very small parts, making it capable of producing exact replicas of the original performance in other instruments. Not all instruments have all the features listed above, and there are also a few more elements yet to be discussed. But each instrument will work in some capacity within a MIDI system. As you will see in the next chapters, MIDI is a powerful and well-designed system that does not sacrifice simplicity and ease of use for its abilities.

Early amplifier design - now illegal in most states.

Chapter 4

From Bits to Bach

Synthesizer technology and computer technology are very closely related. It is the microcomputer chip that makes modern electronic instruments sound so good while being so easy to use. Using computer technology does not make things more complex. In fact, it makes working with instruments much simpler. Without the microchips that go inside instruments, it would be impossible to retrieve a stored sound at the touch of a button as most MIDI instruments will do. It would be impossible to have a drum machine or a sequencer. It would be impossible to have a visual display on an instrument to assist in the creating of new sounds. It would be impossible to "sample" sounds. Most kinds of sound processing *(delay, reverb, etc.)* could not be. MIDI would not exist.

Is it important to know how computers operate in order to work with synthesizers and MIDI? No, but the fact is that if you have ever worked with synthesizers, drum machines, sequencers, digital effects, or most any electronic music equipment, you do know how to work with computers, because that's exactly what you are

doing. The image that most people have of computers is of machines with typewriter keyboards and TV screens that do spreadsheets and word processing. This is but one type of computer, known as a personal computer (or PC). With synthesizers, you are simply working with a *different type of computer* in a different way — instead of producing mailing lists, they produce music.✳

The technology behind PCs and MIDI instruments is the same. Computers of any sort have a microprocessor (the brain), digital memory, and some way of sending and receiving information. The sending and receiving function can either be between the computer and people, or between the computer and another machine. For example, a button pressed on the front panel of a synthesizer will cue the internal computer to do something such as change to a different sound or change the current sound in some way. The computer can then display the new sound's name or changed parameter on the synthesizer's front panel. The memory inside the instrument will also have changed.

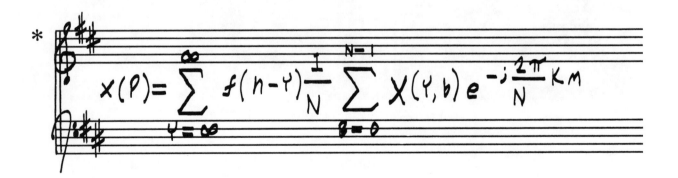

Calling up a program (also called a *patch*) causes the synthesizer to look inside a particular part of its memory to get the various parameters of the sound and then move them to an area to be played or changed. When a key is pressed on the keyboard of a synthesizer, it presses a button that the computer will interpret to mean "play this note now!" The computer will then create a code to send out the MIDI OUT port as well as trigger the synthesizer's sound-producing circuitry to make a sound.

This all leads up to a brief explanation of a few key parts of computer technology that apply directly to MIDI. *MIDI is the sending and receiving of information between two computers;* not the kind that do square roots, but the kind that make music.

Inside The Computer

Computers use electricity to do everything they do. Like any type of electrical circuit, they move electricity around in a very organized manner. The memory inside a computer is a chip of silicon that can store electricity in patterns. Those patterns create a code that only computers can understand. It is the role of the computer to convert those patterns of electricity into information that humans can understand.

Figure 4-1

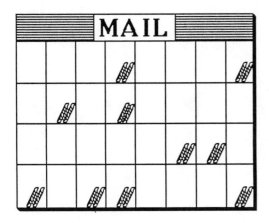

⦚ = Electricity here (bits)

A computer's memory is filled with microscopic pockets that can be filled with a bit of electricity or can be empty as shown in Figure 4-1. These are the "bits" discussed earlier. A bit will either be ON or OFF depending on whether or not its "mailbox" has any electricity in it. The bits are turned on and off by the computer, which, as was said before, only moves electricity around.

Since the people who invented computers were mathematicians, they were more comfortable thinking of the bits as being either 1 (for ON) or 0 (for OFF). The two values for a single bit, 1 and 0, are used by most people working with computers. While this is one of the great technical accomplishments of the Twentieth Century, being able to count up to only 1 is not very useful. To remedy this problem, the bits are combined into groups to represent larger numbers. These groups are called *bytes: A byte is a group of eight bits.*

In our standard counting system there are ten different digits (0-9), and each number column is ten times greater than the one next to it:

Figure 4-2

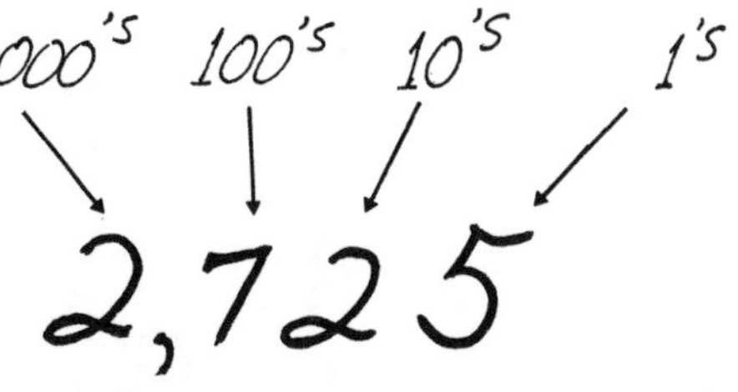

$$\overset{1,000\text{'s}\quad 100\text{'s}\quad 10\text{'s}\qquad 1\text{'s}}{2,725}$$

In computer memory counting there are only two different digits (0 and 1), and each number column is *two times* greater than the number column next to it:

Figure 4-3

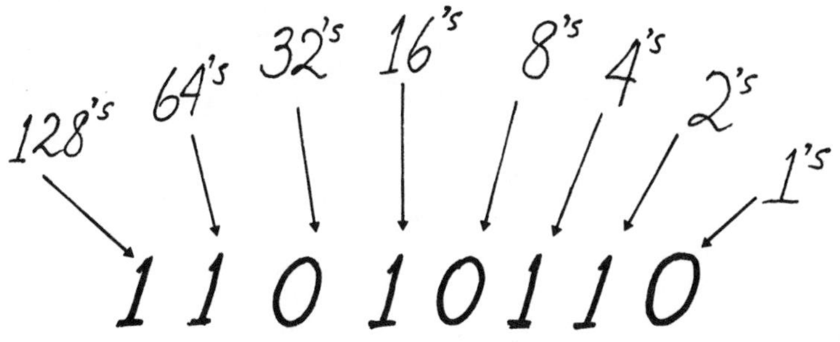

$$\overset{128\text{'s}\quad 64\text{'s}\quad 32\text{'s}\quad 16\text{'s}\quad 8\text{'s}\quad 4\text{'s}\quad 2\text{'s}\quad 1\text{'s}}{1\ 1\ 0\ 1\ 0\ 1\ 1\ 0}$$

A group of eight bits can represent values from 0 to 255. This number comes from adding all the number columns together (255 = 128 + 64 + 32 + 16 + 8 + 4 + 2 + 1). Though a byte is just a group of eight 0s or 1s inside the computer, it's the computer's job (with the help of software) to convert those bytes into all kinds of information — including letters, numbers, symbols, graphics, and commands. Musical instruments use bytes to represent program settings, front panel knob and button settings, keys pressed, rhythmic patterns in a drum machine and anything else the synthesizer will do or remember.

Like the symbols in hieroglyphics, the dots and dashes of Morse code, or the tones in a Touch Tone phone, the bytes in a computer are a code. MIDI information is a computer code as well. Every time a key is pressed or a pitch wheel is moved, one or more bytes is sent out the MIDI OUT port. Other synthesizers connected to that sending instrument are looking for those bytes to come over the wire, which are then interpreted back into commands for the synthesizer to obey. It is not a complex concept, and you certainly don't need a computer background to understand or use it.

Perhaps the most important idea to grasp is that *MIDI does not send or receive sounds.* There is no audio going through a MIDI cable, only the codes that a synthesizer will use to produce sounds of its own.

This chapter has introduced the idea of computer codes, which are made up of *bytes.* This is the form MIDI data takes as it passes from one instrument to another. This information will be referred to often throughout the book.

Chapter 5

The Basics of MIDI

You should now have a fair idea of what bits and bytes are. These are the building blocks of the MIDI code. This chapter shows how these numbers are applied in MIDI.

In order for MIDI to get the most mileage out of an eight-bit number system (which can only count from 0 to 255), MIDI bytes come in two flavors, called *status* and *data:*

Status bytes describe the *kind* of information being sent. They tell the other instruments whether this is a key press, a pitch wheel, or another type of action. This is the first byte sent by a MIDI instrument when an action occurs.

Data bytes follow status bytes and indicate the actual *values* of the event. If the status byte indicated a key press (Note On), then the following data bytes would indicate which key was pressed, and the velocity with which it was struck. A status byte is followed by one or more data bytes, depending on the type of information being sent.

Status and data bytes can be distinguished in MIDI by the value of the highest (leftmost) bit. When this top bit is on (1), then the byte is a status byte. If the top bit is off (0), then the byte is a data byte. This top bit on/off scheme makes the decoding of MIDI information easier for any receiving instruments.

Figure 5-1

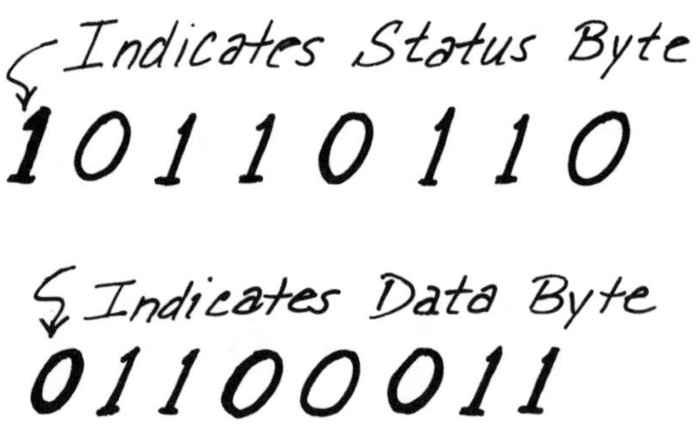

Indicates Status Byte
1 0 1 1 0 1 1 0

Indicates Data Byte
0 1 1 0 0 0 1 1

A good analogy for thinking about status and data in MIDI is a train made up of an engine with a couple of cars attached:

Figure 5-2

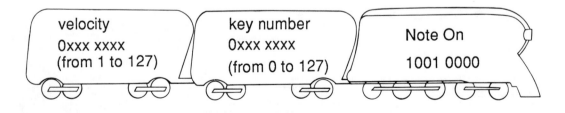

velocity
0xxx xxxx
(from 1 to 127)

key number
0xxx xxxx
(from 0 to 127)

Note On
1001 0000

The train's engine in the drawing above represents the *status* byte sent by a MIDI instrument when a note is played on it. It is recognized by a receiving instrument as a status byte because the top bit is a 1.

The cars of the train are the *data* bytes that immediately follow the status byte. They go on to give the actual values of the event. A status byte alone has no information in it about the event it signals, only the basic *nature* of the event (a key pressed, a wheel moved, etc.). The data bytes give the values, but require the status byte to tell the receiving instruments exactly what the data bytes are describing. Later on you will see that there are some situations in which it is permitted to send some data bytes without first sending the status byte every time.

MIDI Channels

MIDI has made possible the creation of *electronic music systems* — many instruments working together to create the final sound. Sounds can be layered on top of one another with multiple instruments, and sequencers make it possible for each instrument to play a different part. This is accomplished through the use of *channels* in MIDI. Different musical parts, each meant to be played on different instruments, can be transmitted together over the same MIDI cable. Each part will be played back by a synthesizer that is set to the same channel.

Figure 5-3

As a similar example, cable television can have literally hundreds of stations' signals broadcast over a single cable at once. A tuner that is connected to the TV set can select one channel at a time and ignore all the rest. Each station broadcasts on a separate frequency, and the TV's tuner acts as a filter to let only one station's frequency pass.

Channels are used in MIDI to make it possible for each instrument in a system to play unique parts while connected together by a single MIDI cable. Instead of using frequencies like TV or radio, MIDI uses one half of the *status byte* to indicate the channel of the data that follows it:

Figure 5-4

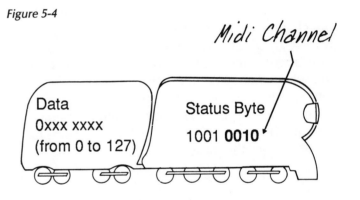

As was mentioned earlier, if a MIDI byte has a top bit of 1, it is called a *status* byte and it tells the receiving synthesizer the kind of information that will follow. *The lower four bits of the status byte specify the MIDI channel.* Four bits (also called a "nibble") have 16 possible values (0 to 15), and so MIDI has 16 channels available:

Binary	MIDI Channel	Binary	MIDI Channel
0000	channel 1	1000	channel 9
0001	channel 2	1001	channel 10
0010	channel 3	1010	channel 11
0011	channel 4	1011	channel 12
0100	channel 5	1100	channel 13
0101	channel 6	1101	channel 14
0110	channel 7	1110	channel 15
0111	channel 8	1111	channel 16

Figure 5-7 A Synthesizer's Channel Selector

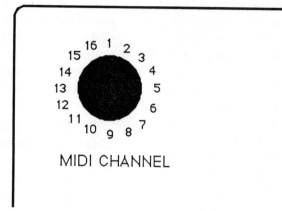

MIDI CHANNEL

Most MIDI synthesizers have a way to select the channel number on which it will send and receive MIDI data. When anything is played on the instrument, each transmitted status byte will have the selected channel number in the lowest four bits. Other instruments that are set to the same channel will respond and play the incoming data. Instruments set to other channels will receive, but simply ignore the information.

A MIDI sequencer can record and store MIDI data from all sixteen channels and play them all back at the same time over one cable connected to its MIDI OUT port. The information for the various channels will be mixed together. A receiving instrument can ignore incoming information from other channels while playing the part on the channel to which it is set.

Figure 5-8

Channels give MIDI a great deal of power and versatility. Without them, every instrument would play all the time. Since all sixteen channels can be transmitted over a single cable, you won't necessarily need to get into a bad case of *electro-spaghetti* with separate cables from a source to each instrument and always need to be to unplug-

ging and replugging everything. When the status byte comes to a synthesizer that is set to a different channel, the instrument knows to ignore all the data (the cars on the train) until the next status byte comes along. It will then check again to see if this is information on the channel to which it is set. It will continue to do this with all incoming MIDI data.

Since most MIDI instruments send on a single MIDI channel at a time, changing the MIDI channel makes it possible to select one from a number of "slave" synthesizers that are attached. This way you can turn other synthesizers on and off at the touch of a button from the "master" keyboard

Figure 5-9

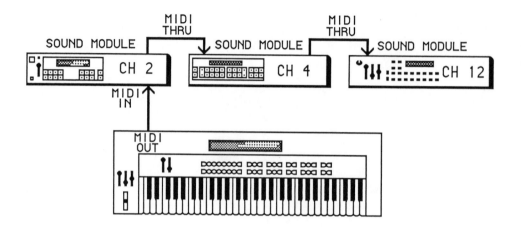

Hexadecimal — The Computer Counting System

There is a numbering system often used in computers and MIDI that will be referred to from time to time in the remainder of this book. It is called *hexadecimal* numbering. It is a standard for computer systems. No, you will not be expected to be an expert in odd counting systems, but parts of MIDI are easier to read in hexadecimal. Hexadecimal works in *base sixteen.* Just as there are ten digits in our standard base ten numbering system (0 to 9), and two digits (0 and 1) in the binary system seen earlier, there are sixteen different digits in hexadecimal. Letters are used to represent the digits above 9.

Here is a chart showing the relationship between decimal (base 10) and hexadecimal (base 16):

Hexadecimal	Decimal
00	0
01	1
02	2
03	3
04	4
05	5
06	6
07	7
08	8
09	9
0A	10
0B	11
0C	12
0D	13
0E	14
0F	15

The chart above shows the first sixteen digits of the hexadecimal counting system. In *decimal* numbers, each column is *ten* times greater than the one to its right (1s, 10s, 100s, etc.). Similarly, with *hexadecimal* numbers, each column is *sixteen* times greater than the one to its right (1s, 16s, 128s, 256s, etc.). It is typical to place a zero in front of a single-digit hexadecimal number. For example, the hexadecimal number 8 will be shown as 08. It does not change its value in any way. At times throughout this book you will see numbers that have letters A to F in them, followed by the letter H. The H indicates that these are numbers in hexadecimal notation. For example, the number 127 in decimal is 7FH in hexadecimal (7x16 + 15x1 = 112 + 15 = 127).

Certain details of MIDI messages are clearer when displayed in hexadecimal. The most important one is channels. As we have seen, there are sixteen channels in MIDI, which are represented in the lower four bits of a MIDI status byte. It is possible to show which channel a MIDI message is on with a *single* hexadecimal digit, because it has sixteen possible values.

So by showing a MIDI byte in hexadecimal, you can easily see the channel number by looking at its lower digit. Because people begin counting with the number 1 rather than 0, the actual MIDI channel number is always one higher than the hexadecimal code number.

As an example, the MIDI code for a Note On event on Channel 1 is 90H (hexadecimal). The first digit, the 9, is the MIDI code for a Note On. The second digit, the 0, is the MIDI channel, which is set to Channel 1. A Note On on MIDI Channel 2 would be 91H, a Note On on MIDI Channel 3 would be 92H, and so on. So a MIDI status byte that is displayed in hexadecimal can be split into two parts, the type of message represented in the first digit and the channel number represented in the second digit.

Hexa-decimal	Channel Number
00	Channel 1
01	Channel 2
02	Channel 3
03	Channel 4
04	Channel 5
05	Channel 6
06	Channel 7
07	Channel 8
08	Channel 9
09	Channel 10
0A	Channel 11
0B	Channel 12
0C	Channel 13
0D	Channel 14
0E	Channel 15
0F	Channel 16

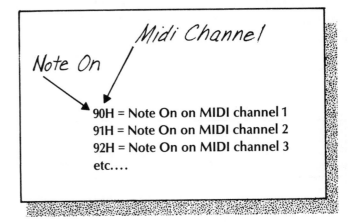

Note On / Midi Channel

90H = Note On on MIDI channel 1
91H = Note On on MIDI channel 2
92H = Note On on MIDI channel 3
etc....

Throughout this book, and in other MIDI data as well, there is a standard way of writing a MIDI status message without its channel, if the channel is not important: If a Note On message is shown, but the channel is not important, it will be written as "9n." The lowercase "n" takes the place of the channel number. In fact "n" stands for "number." When you see this, it simply means "a Note On on any MIDI channel."

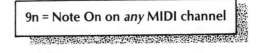

9n = Note On on *any* MIDI channel

Chapter 6

An Overview of MIDI

With an understanding of the nature of codes, it is time to take a look at the MIDI code itself. Different words have been used to define what MIDI is — it has been called a code, a language, a protocol, a standard, and a specification. All of these definitions are fine. The word MIDI is used to describe *both* the information being sent and the way it is sent. Each aspect of a musical performance is represented by its own code number and format. These formats are rigidly adhered to in the musical instrument industry.

Following is a table with the definition and format for all MIDI commands. The status byte is shown in hexadecimal. The lowercase "n" is in place of the channel number in the status byte. Data bytes are shown in normal decimal notation. The chapters following the table will explain each of the codes in greater detail.

Channel Voice Messages

These are the basis of MIDI. They are for transmitting information about a musical performance:

STATUS BYTE	DATA BYTES	DEFINITION
8n	1: key number 2: velocity	Note Off
9n	1: key number 2: velocity	Note On
An	1: key number 2: pressure amount	Polyphonic Key Pressure (Aftertouch)
Bn	1: controller number 2: control value	Control Change
Cn	1: program number	Program Change
Dn	1: pressure value	Channel Pressure (Aftertouch)
En	1: pitch bend (course) 2: pitch bend (fine)	Pitch Bend Change

Channel Mode Messages

Channel Modes tell a synthesizer to send or receive data a certain way. Channel Mode messages all use the Control Change status byte. The first data byte defines the particular mode being sent:

STATUS BYTE	DATA BYTES	DEFINITION
Bn	1: #122 2: 1 = On / 0 = Off	Local Control
	1: #123 2: 0	All Notes Off
	1: #124 2: 0	Omni Mode Off
	1: #125 2: 0	Omni Mode On
	1: #126 2: number of channels 3: 0	Mono Mode On
	1: #127 2: 0	Poly Mode On

System Common Messages

These messages enhance the functions of other MIDI commands. Because they are "common," they do not have channels.

STATUS BYTE	DATA BYTES	DEFINITION
F1	1: frame number	MTC (MIDI Time Code)
F2	1: position (Least Significant Byte) 2: position (Most Significant Byte)	Song Position Pointer
F3	1: song number	Song Select
F4		Undefined
F5		Undefined
F6	(none)	Tune Request
F7	(none)	End of Exclusive Message

System Real Time Messages

These commands are used for synchronizing parts of a MIDI system. They do not have channel numbers.

STATUS BYTE	DATA BYTES	DEFINITION
F8	(none)	Timing Clock
F9	(none)	Undefined
FA	(none)	Start
FB	(none)	Continue
FC	(none)	Stop
FD	(none)	Undefined
FE	(none)	Active Sensing
FF	(none)	System Reset

System Exclusive Messages

These messages are primarily used for dumping the memory of an instrument to another of the same instrument.

STATUS BYTE	DATA BYTES	DEFINITION
F0	1: identification	System Exclusive
	2-??: (there may be any number of data bytes here)	
F7	(none)	End of Exclusive

Use these tables as reference guides to each MIDI code number. The next chapters go into detail on each message. As you can see, MIDI is made up of a rather small number of command messages. Looking at them grouped by function will help you see the logic behind MIDI.

Chapter 7

Channel Voice Messages

The most basic commands in MIDI are the *Channel Voice Messages.* These messages communicate the most often used performance events sent from one instrument to another over any of the sixteen MIDI channels. MIDI is capable of representing and reproducing nearly every subtle nuance that even an advanced player can perform. Yet the hardware and commands used to do this are actually quite simple.

channel as the sending instrument — the one being played — will respond by playing the same notes. There are two bytes of data that follow a Note On status byte: the *first one* tells the *key number* (0 to 127), and the *second one* is the *velocity with which the key is struck* (1 to 127). A Note On looks like this when it is sent:

Figure 7-2

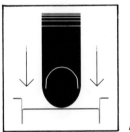

Note On

Figure 7-1

| velocity
63H
01100011 | key number
40H
01000000 | Note On
90H
1001 0000 |

| velocity
0xxx xxxx
(from 1 to 127) | key number
0xxx xxxx
(from 0 to 127) | Note On
9nH
1001 xxxx
(from 0 to 15) |

The most basic activity in any musical performance is the playing of notes. MIDI uses two separate messages, *Note On* and *Note Off,* to represent the playing of notes. That is, one MIDI instrument will send Note On and Note Off messages to another instrument, which will in turn play those same notes. These note messages are sent over one of the 16 MIDI channels. Note messages are, therefore, considered to be Channel Messages. Any other instrument set to the same MIDI

The Note On shown above is on MIDI channel 1 (the "0" in the status byte 90H). It is a middle "C" on the keyboard (40H hexadecimal or 64 decimal), and is fairly loud (63 out of possible 7F in hexadecimal, or 99 out of 127 in decimal).

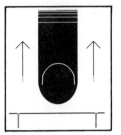

Note Off

As shown in the MIDI chart in the previous chapter, there is a separate command for Note Off, though this is rarely used in MIDI. Instead, when a key is released, a Note On command is usully sent again with the same pitch but with a velocity of 0 (no volume). A velocity of 0 is used to represent "a key has been released." The Note Off command (8n) is typically used only when the synthesizer has the ability to sense *Release Velocity* (how quickly a key is released), and uses it to determine the speed of the release *envelope* (the synthesizer parameter that determines how quickly a note begins and ends). This is quite rare among most synthesizer keyboards. Note Offs are therefore rarely seen passing through the average MIDI cable.

Key Numbers

Key numbers are used to represent each key of the keyboard. There are 128 possible keys in a MIDI instrument. This is more than sufficient since it is rare to find a keyboard with more than 88 keys. The lowest note number, "0," is "C" five octaves below middle "C." The lowest note found on a piano is two octaves higher — key number 24. After key 0 comes key number 1 (C#), key number 2 (D), etc. Key number 127 ("G" five octaves above middle "C") is the highest value.

Though key number 60 is middle "C" on a piano keyboard, this does not mean that this number will cause a middle "C" to be played on a synthesizer. The particular patch (sound on a synthesizer) the synthesizer is set to could be producing any pitch at all, or even no pitch if it is a sound effect. For this reason, it is incorrect to say that MIDI sends pitches. It does not. It simply sends the key number that was pressed by the player. It is the synthesizer's sound settings that will determine the pitch that results from a key press or MIDI Note On message.

Figure 7-3 MIDI Range

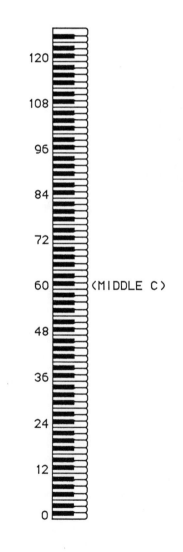

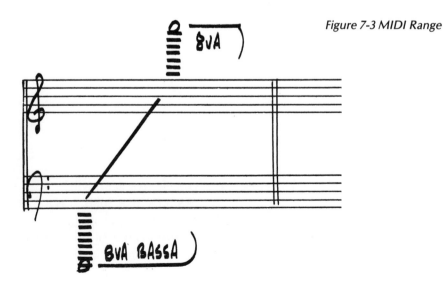

Velocity

After the key number is sent in a Note On message, a byte is sent to show how *fast* (the velocity) the key was pressed. This is usually translated into how loud the note will sound on the receiving instrument. The very lowest possible velocity is 1, which would be interpreted as *"ppp"* or *pianissimo* in musical terms — very quiet. The highest value is 127, which would be like *"fff"* or *fortissimo* in music — very, very loud. A velocity of 0 would represent the releasing of a key, or "no volume."

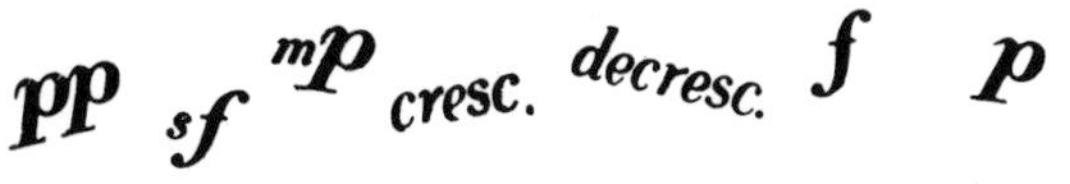

pp *sf* *mp* *cresc.* *decresc.* *f* *p*

Of course in synthesis, velocity can be used for parameters other than just loudness. It can be used to make a sound brighter, higher, lower, "bendier," or to completely change the sound from the way it might be if played softly. For this reason, it is always referred to as "velocity" in MIDI and never "loudness" or "volume."

Velocity is not a separate command in MIDI. It is part of the data linked with every Note On message. It cannot be omitted from Note On or Note Off messages. Keyboards that are not velocity sensitive use a "dummy" value of 64 for the velocity byte. This value is exactly in the middle of the dynamic range of MIDI.

Here is a musical example in standard music notation and then as it would appear in MIDI code:

Figure 7-4

90H	3EH	21H	Note On, key number 62 (D), mezzo-piano
90H	3EH	00H	Note Off (velocity 0), key number 62 (D)
90H	41H	40H	Note On, key number 65 (F), louder
90H	45H	42H	Note On, key number 69 (A)
90H	41H	00H	Note Off (velocity 0), key number 65 (F)
90H	45H	00H	Note Off (velocity 0), key number 69 (A)
90H	48H	65H	Note On, key number 72 (C), forte
90H	40H	71H	Note On, key number 64 (E), forte
90H	40H	00H	Note Off (velocity 0), key number 64 (E)
90H	48H	00H	Note Off (velocity 0), key number 72 (C)

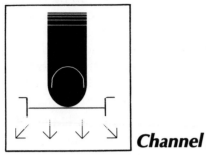

Channel Aftertouch

Figure 7-5

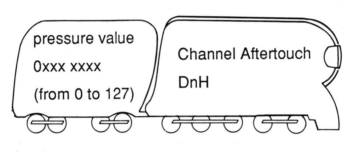

pressure value

0xxx xxxx

(from 0 to 127)

Channel Aftertouch

DnH

In addition to sensing the speed with which a key is depressed, many MIDI keyboards also have a sensor underneath the key bed to sense if a key is pressed down even harder after it has been struck. This parameter is called *aftertouch,* though "afterpress" might describe it better. Another term used is *"channel key pressure."* The sensor reads a single value for the entire keyboard, and whichever key is being pressed the hardest will determine the aftertouch value sent out through MIDI. As a key is pressed harder and harder, higher and higher values are transmitted. If a key is not touched, or if the pressure is held steady, then no information is sent. Any receiving instrument set to the same MIDI channel will respond to this information if it has the capability to do so.

Aftertouch is usually used for modulation (that's vibrato to you and me). Some synthesizers can use it for other effects, such as volume or brightness. It can be very expressive and is simple to use since it does not involve removing your hands from the keyboard.

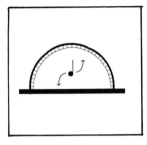

Pitch Bend Change

Figure 7-6

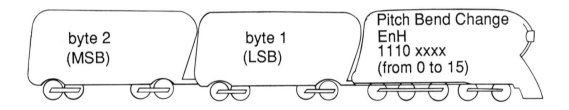

The so-called "blue notes" in jazz and the blues — a slightly sharp dominant seventh and the slightly flat minor third — have for many years been exclusively in the domain of singers, guitarists, wind, and brass players. Keyboardists have tried to approximate the sound of blues with expressive grace notes, but it isn't the same. Electronics have become the stylistic liberation for the keyboard player, since the capability of pitch bending has been added to these instruments. Pitch bend is frequently used by synthesizer players of many styles. It is rare to see a keyboard without a pitch bend wheel or lever. Since this is a major element of the instrument's design, it follows that a portion of MIDI is designed to read the pitch wheel and send information about its position to other instruments so they can replicate it.

The human ear is very critical when it comes to pitch and can hear the difference between a tone that is gliding and one that is moving in steps. Since digital instruments work in steps, it is very important that the steps be very, very small. The code for pitch bend wheels uses not one, but two bytes of information, so there are 16,384 steps from the lowest position to the highest. If pitch bend were to use only a single byte to send the position data, there would only be 128 possible positions, and the steps between them would be audible to most people.

Any other MIDI instrument that is capable of pitch bend, and is set to the same MIDI channel on which you are sending pitch bend information, will bend its notes also. However, it is possible that the sensitivity of the pitch bend function on the receiving instrument may be different than that of the sending instrument. While the sending instrument may bend up or down a major second, the receiving one may move a fifth or an entire octave. It is normal for this parameter to be programmable for each sound in a synthesizer. There is a recently added controller code in MIDI to set the sensitivity of pitch bend in an instrument, but it is still rarely used. It is the responsibility of the player to be sure that the pitch bend ranges of all the instruments in the system are matched.

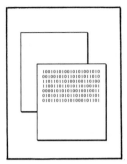

Program Change

Figure 7-7

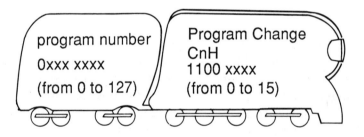

program number

0xxx xxxx

(from 0 to 127)

Program Change
CnH
1100 xxxx
(from 0 to 15)

The patch memories inside MIDI instruments are called *programs.* Any instrument with memory has at least a few. When you press a patch button on the front of an instrument, two things happen: First, the instrument gets the sound you want out of memory and prepares it to play. Second, it sends the *number of the patch* you selected through MIDI. Instruments set to the same MIDI channel on which you are sending will go to the same patch number if they have it.

Remember, just the *number* of the program is sent, not the parameters of the sound itself. With sequencers, it is possible to have one synthesizer fill a multiple role in a song by changing sounds (patches) at different times during the music. Since the sequencer will record the program changes and play them back, it is possible to automate the changing of sounds in a piece. The instruments in a MIDI system may have different, but complimentary, sounds in the matching memory locations of each one. While pressing a patch button on the master synth will call up one component of an overall sound, the other synthesizers set on the same MIDI channel will call up their own patches to create the final sound. This is an important and valuable use of MIDI.

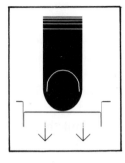

Polyphonic Key Pressure

Figure 7-8

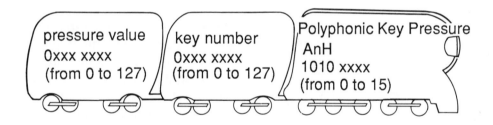

As previously mentioned, the MIDI code for Channel Key Pressure, or Aftertouch, consists of the status byte followed by a single byte of data indicating the amount of pressure being applied to the most heavily pressed key on the keyboard.

With *Polyphonic Key Pressure,* each key can have its own individual pressure level. This adds another level of expression to an instrument, but it does require that the keyboard have an individual pressure sensor under each key. This can add a lot of expense and weight to an instrument and is not often found in MIDI keyboards.

At any rate, there is a separate MIDI code specifically to describe this kind of information. The status byte for Polyphonic Key Pressure, which includes the MIDI channel on which the information is being transmitted, is sent along with a key number, just like Note On or Note Off. But instead of sending a velocity as the third byte, the pressure value for that individual key is sent. For example, a chord can be held while a melody note above it can have vibrato. With Channel Aftertouch, vibrato would be applied to every note just from pressing on the melody note alone.

Summary

These channel messages comprise the majority of MIDI data. The next chapter goes into more detail about Controllers, which are also channel messages. With Note On and Off, Pitch Bend Change, Channel Pressure, Polyphonic Pressure, and Program Change, a whole world is opened up for the musician. It is amazing that with just these six codes, and the ones described in the next chapter, instruments can communicate nearly everything about a musical performance, or even several performances at the same time.

Remember that channel messages are sent over a single channel, and that channel is selected on the instrument that will be sending the information. There is a MIDI channel selector on virtually all MIDI instruments. In MIDI messages the status byte is used to indicate the channel. Only those instruments set to the same channel as the sending instrument will respond to the information being sent. Instruments connected to the sender but set to different channels will receive the data but will ignore it. This way it is not necessary to unplug or turn off an instrument just because you don't wish to use it.

Fast And Faster

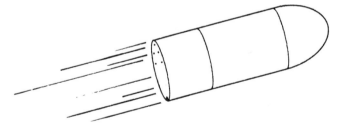

MIDI sends information at a rate of 31,250 bits per second. This speed is called a *baud rate.* Since MIDI is serial (step by step), it sends one bit at a time over a single wire. A MIDI byte consists of 8 bits. Because of the way MIDI ports are designed, there are two additional bits used every time a byte is sent to synchronize the receiving instrument's MIDI IN port, bringing the total up to ten bits per byte. This means that MIDI sends about three bytes of data every *millisecond* (one thousandth of a second).

A Note On message has three bytes in it: the status byte, the key number and the velocity. At the MIDI speed of 31,250 bits per second, a Note On will take .96 milliseconds to be sent. To keep things simple, this can be rounded off and called one millisecond. It will take another three bytes —another millisecond — to shut that note off. If it takes one millisecond to turn the note on and another millisecond to turn the note off, then MIDI can play approximately 500 notes a second. That's fast!

However, the ear is highly sensitive. It can detect if two notes are played simultaneously or if they are slightly apart. How slightly? Many experts feel that when there's a gap of less than 20 to 40 milliseconds between two notes, they will appear to sound together. When the gap is longer, it will start to become perceptible. Some of this will depend on the types of sound being heard. A sound with a fast, clicky attack will be more noticeable if some notes are mistimed than will a slow string or brass sound.

Using the numbers discussed above, it can be assumed that chords played through MIDI should have no trouble being heard as chords. An eight-note chord (eight Note Ons) will take MIDI only eight milliseconds to send. A problem can occur when there are several channels of information being sent simultaneously from a sequencer and there is a large number of controller messages along with the notes. The capabilities of MIDI can be strained to the point of becoming audible. Chords can "spray" slightly or may sound a bit out of rhythm. There is no hard rule to say when or if this will happen in a particular MIDI system, or with a certain kind of music.

This has become a point of major controversy in MIDI. Is it fast enough? Should it be replaced with something faster? One fact that has been determined is that delays occurring in MIDI systems are due more to the instruments themselves than to the way MIDI works. It takes a specific amount of time for an instrument's microprocessor to respond to the MIDI information it receives. As instrument designs improve, these delays are shrinking.

"31,250 bits per second. Not just a good idea — it's the law."

Running Status

What if it were possible to play notes and send other kinds of MIDI information in fewer bytes? The overall efficiency of MIDI would improve. This would mean that more messages could be sent in less time. Eliminating just one byte in a Note On message would speed up the message by 33%. Well, such a scheme does exist, and is used in a large number of instruments and sequencers.

The technique for reducing the number of bytes needed for sending MIDI messages is called *running status.* Every MIDI message has a status byte to indicate the type of message being sent and the MIDI channel of the data. For example, if a four-note chord is played on a keyboard, the MIDI message might look like this:

NOTE 1	NOTE 2	NOTE 3	NOTE 4
90-27-42	90-32-48	90-36-51	90-37-46

The overall message consists of four consecutive Note On messages on MIDI channel 1. It will take nearly four milliseconds to send the entire stream of information. But notice that the status byte is the same for each note. It is a waste of time to send the status byte for every data message if the status is the same for all of them. The idea behind running status is that an instrument will *only send a status byte when the type of data changes.* Now the chord above could be sent this way:

NOTE 1	NOTE 2	NOTE 3	NOTE 4
90-27-42	32-48	36-51	37-46

A status byte is sent at the beginning to show the type of data (Note On) and the channel (channel 1). Since the rest of the messages are the same type and the same channel, the status is *assumed.* Running status has removed three bytes from the message and saved a millisecond of time.

Synthesizers do not usually generate running status while they are being played. Of course there usually isn't a problem of speed when one person is just playing a keyboard (unless he or she wants to play more than 500 notes a second). The problem comes up when several parts have been recorded into a sequencer and are all being played back together. For this reason, most sequencers will intelligently strip away any unneeded status bytes to create running status as they play. Since MIDI data can take up a lot of room inside a sequencer's memory, running status also helps sequencers to hold more music.

Notes are not the biggest time saver when using running status. There usually aren't more than a few dozen notes in a measure of most music. However, moving a pitch bend wheel or using aftertouch can send out hundreds of messages in a very short time. Here, running status becomes of critical importance. The savings in time add up to a big increase in efficiency.

Is MIDI fast enough? For almost everybody, the answer is yes. Are there still improvements to be made in the efficiency of MIDI instruments? While they have gotten considerably better, the answer is yes again. MIDI was designed with the most demanding needs of musicians in mind. Running status was conceived to help achieve those goals. Together they have produced a musical system with the ability to last for years to come.

Chapter 8

MIDI Controllers

I n addition to the pitch bend wheel found on
nearly all MIDI synthesizers, there are other
wheels, buttons, levers, switches or pedals
used for *controlling* some expressive elements of a
synthesizer's performance. Each of these controllers, called "continuous controllers" in MIDI, is
represented by a unique number. When one of
these controllers is moved, the instrument sends
the following message:

Figure 8-1

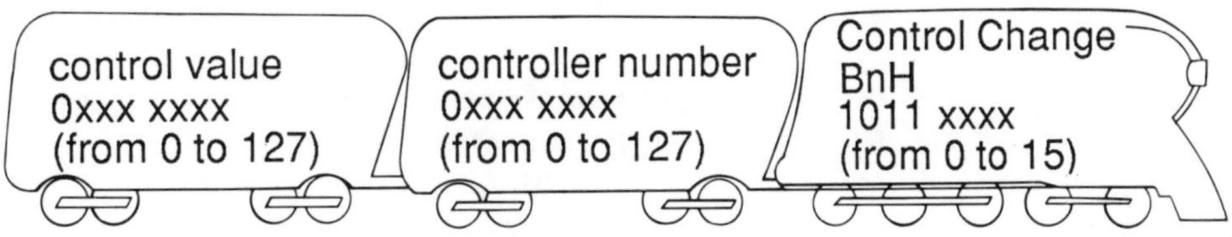

control value	controller number	Control Change
0xxx xxxx	0xxx xxxx	BnH
(from 0 to 127)	(from 0 to 127)	1011 xxxx
		(from 0 to 15)

Instruments set to the same MIDI channel
will respond to these messages in a variety of ways,
some more obvious than others. Controllers such
as modulation wheel, sustain pedal, or portamento
time are fairly obvious in the effect they will have
on a receiving synthesizer. Other controllers, such
as breath controller or data entry may not be as
outwardly clear in their effect on an instrument.
Below is the complete list of MIDI continuous controllers and the numbers assigned to them (as of
this printing). Many of these were added as the
need for more control over a MIDI performance
became obvious. Following the table are brief
explanations of some of the more important features of the controllers found therein.

Controller Number	Definition
0	Undefined
1	Modulation wheel or lever
2	Breath Controller
3	Undefined
4	Foot controller
5	Portamento time
6	Data entry MSB
7	Main volume
8	Balance
9	Undefined
10	Pan
11	Expression Pedal
12-15	Undefined
16-19	General Purpose Controllers
20-31	Undefined
32-37	LSB for values 0-5
38	Data Entry LSB
39-63	LSB for values 7-31
64	Damper pedal (sustain)
65	Portamento
66	Sostenuto
67	Soft pedal
68	Undefined
69	Hold 2
70-79	Undefined
80-83	General Purpose Controllers
84-90	Undefined
91	External Effects Depth
92	Tremelo Depth
93	Chorus Depth
94	Celeste (Detune) Depth
95	Phaser Depth
96	Data increment
97	Data decrement
98	Non-Registered Parameter Number LSB
99	Non-Registered Parameter Number MSB
100	Registered Parameter Number LSB
101	Registered Parameter Number MSB
102-121	Undefined

→ **#0** Interestingly, the list of MIDI controllers begins with room in which to grow. MIDI controller 0 is reserved until a use is decided for it. It may well be used in the future as a "gateway" to a new group of functions.

→ **#1** *Modulation wheel.* This controller is a very common one found on virtually all MIDI instruments. It is a wheel or lever that when moved adds modulation to a sound. Modulation is the term for vibrato, an essential element of musical expression. Modulation can be used to create pitch vibrato (frequency modulation), loudness vibrato (amplitude modulation), brightness vibrato (filter modulation), or special effects. All of these are functions of the synthesizer itself, and are not controlled through MIDI.

→ **#2** The *breath controller* was introduced by Yamaha for the DX7 synthesizer. It is used primarily for exactly the same functions as a modulation wheel. For this reason, while other companies do not make a breath controller, their instruments will respond to its MIDI controller number and use it for some sort of modulation.

→ **#4** The *foot controller* is a universal control which can perform any one of a number of functions. Like the breath controller or the modulation wheel it can be used for vibrato, brightness, etc.

→ **#6** *Data entry* is a way to use MIDI to change the sound of a synthesizer from a remote device. The device can be another synthesizer, a special programmer, or a computer. Many synthesizers use a single slider or dial to change all the parameters of the instrument's sound. The Roland Alpha Dial or the Yamaha Data Entry Slider are examples of these. They are global sound editors for the internal functions of the synthesizer. They send out a code to indicate that they are being moved. Since the control is assigned to any one of a large number of parameters, there is also a MIDI code to indicate the parameter itself. Those codes,

found farther down on the list, are numbered 98 to 101. *Unregistered parameters* are ones for use exclusively with one company's instruments, and are not used for programming other equipment. *Registered parameters* are those potentially universal enough to be used with equipment from different companies.

Controller number 6 is used for parameters with a single byte of data (MSB or Most Significant Byte). If a second byte of data is needed for higher resolution, controller 38 (Data Entry Least Significant Byte) is sent immediately after the controller 6 data.

→ **#7** *Volume* is used to control an instrument's output level from a remote device just as if you were to turn the volume up or down on its own front panel. This can be used to do "MIDI mixing," using instruments that have the ability to respond to this command. While many instruments will respond to MIDI Volume, only a few have a slider or knob to send this parameter. Master volume controls on instruments do not send MIDI volume data.

→ **#32 to #37** *Least Significant Byte (LSB).* It was mentioned earlier that the pitch bend control in MIDI uses two bytes of data instead of one to give smoother control over the bender. Without both bytes it might be possible to hear the little digital steps between the wheel positions. More bytes allows smaller steps, which means the steps will be less perceptible.

With several continuous controllers there is the option of using one byte or using two if it is felt that the higher resolution is needed by the manufacturer. When a single byte is used, it is called the *Most Significant Byte (MSB)*. Using a second byte adds much higher resolution, useful for commands such as modulation or volume. Each of these Least Significant Bytes is preceded by its own controller number. These codes are not often used.

→ **#64** *Sustain Pedal.* Pianos have three pedals — a damper pedal, a soft pedal, and a sostenuto pedal. These are all used in MIDI and each has its own controller number. The most common of these is Controller 64 — *sustain.* It works just like a piano's sustain pedal, allowing notes to continue sounding even after the keys have been released.

→ **#91 to 95** *External Effects Depth, Tremolo Depth, Chorus Depth, Celeste (Detune) Depth, Phaser Depth.* These are used to control external sound processing effects through the use of a MIDI-controlled effects loop on a mixer or amplifier, or to set these effects on instruments which have them built in.

→ **#98-101** *Non-registered and Registered parameters.* While MIDI was not originally intended to control the timbre of an instrument directly, this attitude has changed somewhat. Specific types of "universal" controls — such as filter, envelope, or pitch bend range — will be assigned parameter numbers and will send their current position when changed. These will be used by instruments with special types of controls, such as joysticks.

As with the other channel messages in MIDI, the continuous controllers are sent on a single MIDI channel and will only cause a response in instruments set to the same channel. Further, a particular controller may not be present in certain instruments. In this case, a receiving instrument will simply ignore messages for the controllers it doesn't have. Although there are some MIDI controllers for setting the sensitivity of other controllers, these are rare. The amount of modulation added by a breath controller or modulation wheel and the effect that a foot controller or data slider will have is set up on the individual synthesizer, and is often programmed into each patch memory of the instrument.

The list of controllers goes up to number 121. The controller numbers from 122 to 127 are reserved for very special functions. They are called *Mode Messages* and are used to make the receiving synthesizer respond in different ways to incoming MIDI data. The next chapter deals with these messages in greater detail.

Chapter 9

Mode Messages

polyphonic synthesizer scans its keyboard and relays information about key presses to a computer inside the instrument, which then assigns available oscillators to the keys pressed. In both analog and digital synthesizers, there are often several modes for doing this voice assignment: One mode may assign several oscillators to a single key for a bigger sound, while another mode will make the synthesizer monophonic for a smaller, more intimate sound. Another mode may split the keyboard so that keys pressed on one half of the keyboard will use one patch, while those pressed on the other half will sound completely different.

MIDI has four modes used to decide exactly how a synthesizer will react to incoming note information. These are called *Channel Mode Messages* and, like the other MIDI controllers, work only with instruments set to the appropriate MIDI channel. Not all instruments have all modes. An instrument usually works only in one or two of the modes. The modes break down into two categories, *Omni* and *Poly*.

The omni (meaning "all") modes determine whether a synthesizer will respond to data on a single MIDI channel or to data on all channels. In *Omni On* mode, a receiving instrument will play all incoming MIDI information, regardless of the MIDI channel. In *Omni Off* mode, an instrument responds only to information on the single channel to which it is set — called an instrument's *basic channel*.

It is not unusual to have a synthesizer first power up into the Omni On mode. This makes it easier to connect two instruments together and begin playing without being concerned about the channel to which either one is set. In either Omni On or Omni Off, an instrument will assign all available voices to the messages received.

The two *poly modes* (poly is short for polyphonic) are used to tell a synthesizer how to assign its internal voices (oscillators) to incoming MIDI information. The two modes are called Poly and Mono. In Poly Mode, incoming note messages are assigned to multiple voices in the synthesizer. That is, notes that come into the synthesizer from MIDI will be played polyphonically up to the number of voices the instrument has. This is the most typical way a synthesizer responds to incoming note information. In Mono Mode, incoming note messages are assigned to individual monophonic voices. It is like turning a polyphonic synthesizer into a bunch of monophonic synthesizers, each one able to have its own preset and MIDI channel.

By combining the two Omni modes with the Poly/Mono modes, there are four possible MIDI channel modes. They are:

> MODE 1 : OMNI ON / POLY
> MODE 2 : OMNI ON / MONO
> MODE 3 : OMNI OFF / POLY
> MODE 4 : OMNI OFF / MONO

Figure 9-1

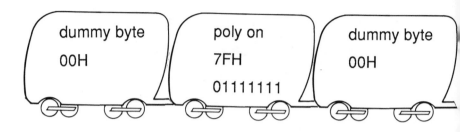

Mode 1 : Omni On / Poly

Omni On/Poly is the mode in which many MIDI instruments power up. In this mode, a synthesizer will play MIDI data received from *any* of the 16 MIDI channels polyphonically. There is no need to be concerned with setting the MIDI channel of the sender or the receiver just to hear the receiver respond to the MIDI data from the sender. This mode is fine for layering or combining the sounds of many synthesizers. It can't be used when a MIDI system is set up to have each synthesizer play a different part; in that case, you want each synthesizer to respond to only a single MIDI channel.

Figure 9-2

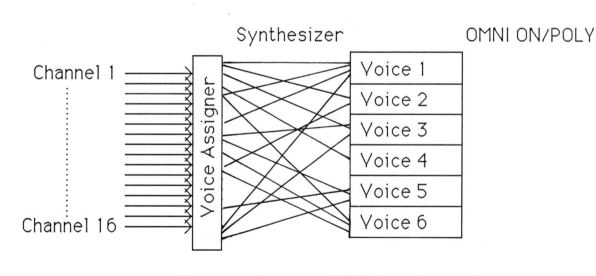

Messages from any MIDI channel are played by all the voices in a synthesizer.

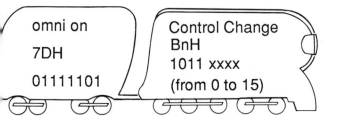

Mode 3 : Omni Off / Poly

The most common mode used in MIDI is Mode 3: Omni Off / Poly, which allows the voices in a synthesizer to play the incoming MIDI information on a single MIDI channel polyphonically. As opposed to Mode 1, though, the receiving instrument will respond only to the incoming information on the one channel to which it is set. MIDI synthesizers all have a way of selecting the MIDI channel to which they will respond — you will find either a rotary knob with the numbers 1 to 16 on it, a display window with a slider control, or buttons with the MIDI channels marked. By setting the instrument to the desired MIDI channel, incoming data on the other 15 channels will be ignored. You always set the MIDI channel of an instrument manually on the instrument itself. *There is no command in MIDI to tell an instrument to change its MIDI channel.*

Figure 9-3

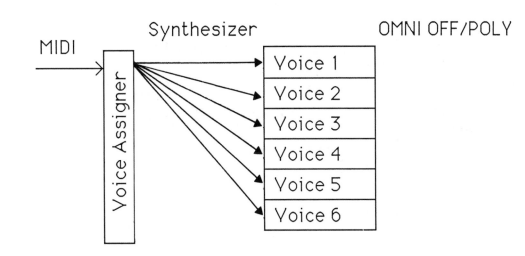

Messages from a single MIDI channel are played by all the voices in a synthesizer.

Mode 4 : Omni Off / Mono

Though much less used, this mode is no less useful. When an instrument is put into Omni Off/Mono mode, it is effectively split into a number of monophonic instruments. This number is usually determined by the number of voices the instrument has. Each voice will respond to a different MIDI channel, and will play a single note at a time when it is received on that channel.

This mode can be useful for synthesizers that are capable of playing many different sounds at once. Such instruments are called *multitimbral* (able to play more than one patch at a time) and, as such, have a very "split" personality. When an instrument is set to Omni Off/Mono, each voice becomes an independent monophonic synthesizer that will respond to its very own MIDI channel.

For example, if you have a six-voice synthesizer in Omni Off/Mono mode set to MIDI channel 4 (the instrument's *basic channel*), it will respond to the six channels 4, 5, 6, 7, 8, and 9. Each voice of the synthesizer takes its own MIDI channel and plays monophonically. What makes this different from the more standard Poly mode is that each voice can have individual pitch bend, MIDI volume, or aftertouch. If the instrument is multitimbral, each voice can play with a different preset sound as well. In poly mode, a pitch bend or other controller would affect all the notes being played on that channel.

Figure 9-4

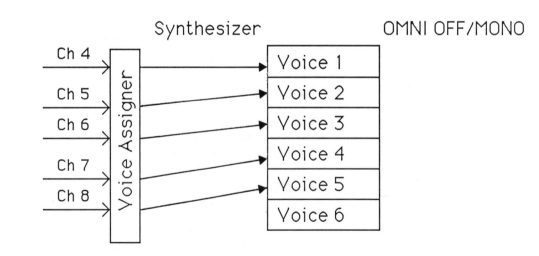

A single note in a MIDI channel is played by one voice in the synthesizer.

Mode 2 : Omni On / Mono

This mode is the least useful, and also least used of the four MIDI modes. A synthesizer will accept messages from any channel (Omni) but it becomes just like a monophonic synthesizer, never playing more than one note at a time. This mode was not part of the original MIDI specification, but a major manufacturer misunderstood Mode 4 and put this on a very popular synthesizer by mistake. This extra mode was added to accommodate the situation and may occasionally find its way to other instruments.

Figure 9-5

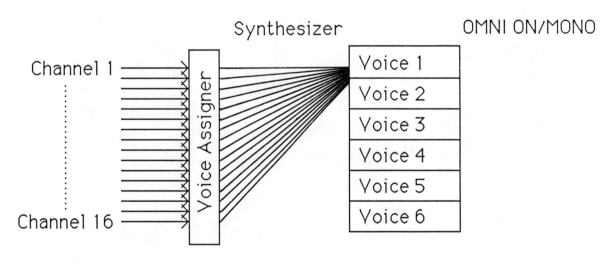

Messages from any MIDI channel are played monophonically by a single voice in the synthesizer.

Setting Modes

A synthesizer's mode may be changed either by a switch on its front panel or by receiving a command over MIDI. These modes are descriptions of how a synthesizer will *receive* a MIDI message. It makes no sense to speak of a synthesizer sending data in Omni Off or Omni On. A Channel Message is always sent on a single channel. This is because a MIDI status byte only has room to indicate a single channel in its lower four bits. A sending instrument could, however, be Mono or Poly. It is possible, for example, to have a MIDI guitar send on six different MIDI channels so that each string can send an individual pitch bend on its own MIDI channel. This is a lot less practical on a keyboard, though it can be done.

The four available modes for MIDI instruments add enormous versatility to a MIDI system. The ability to choose between responding-to-all-channels and responding-to-a-single-channel, or to have many presets playing at once, gives you a great deal more value for your musical investment.

Guitar synthesizers take full advantage of MIDI modes.

Real Time Messages

MIDI instruments can be divided into two basic categories: those instruments with *clocks* and those without. Clocks are used by MIDI sequencers and drum machines to specify and maintain a tempo. A problem that occurred frequently in the past was the synchronization of two or more clock-based machines, such as occurred when linking a sequencer to a drum machine or another sequencer. The reason for

problems in connecting these machines is in the different ways the clocks in them have been implemented.

In order for a sequencer to reproduce a performance accurately, it must time incoming musical events accurately. A tempo is set on the sequencer, usually measured in beats per minute. Each beat is divided into a number of small parts.

Figure 10-1

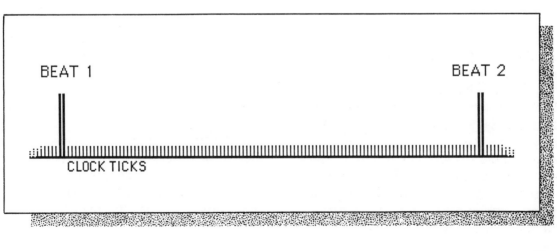

Just as a metronome divides a minute into a specific number of beats, a sequencer divides a beat into a specific number of clock ticks. There are a few names given to these sequencer clock ticks: *timebase, clock rate, resolution, or PPQ (parts per quarternote).* At each one of these clock ticks the sequencer will "look" at the MIDI IN port to see if any messages have come in.

Figure 10-2

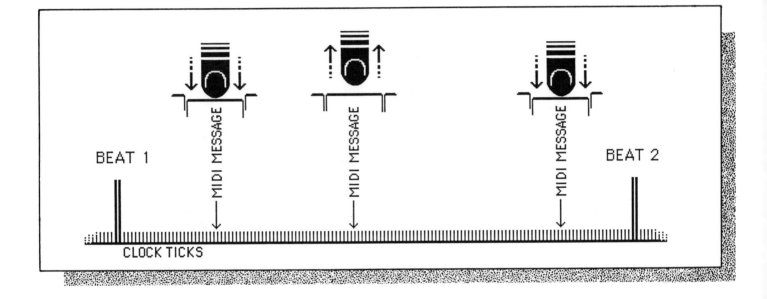

If a MIDI message has entered the sequencer from some MIDI instrument, the sequencer will record it along with the clock tick number. When the sequencer is playing back MIDI data it will use the same clock tick number to know when to play the message. A sequencer will always use the same number of clock ticks for each beat. Sequencers that have more clock ticks for each beat — a higher timebase — will be able to record the timing and rhythms of incoming MIDI data more accurately.

In order for two machines to synchronize, they must share a single clock. One machine acts as a *master* and provides clocking to the other unit, known as the *slave.* In the past, different machines — both drum machines and sequencers — used different timebases for their clocks. Some used 24 PPQ, while others used 48 or 96 PPQ. Additionally, some instruments would use a quarter inch jack to send clock out, while other devices used multi-pin cables similar to a MIDI cable.

One of MIDI's jobs is to remove incompatibilities between musical instruments, including the clock-based ones such as sequencers and drum machines. Instead of using simple electrical pulses as found in earlier clock-based instruments, MIDI uses special codes to synchronize instruments from any manufacturer. These codes are called *System Real Time* messages. Here is a complete list of them:

MIDI Real Time Messages

STATUS BYTE	DATA BYTES	DEFINITION
F8	(none)	Timing Clock
F9	(none)	Undefined
FA	(none)	Start
FB	(none)	Continue
FC	(none)	Stop
FD	(none)	Undefined
FE	(none)	Active Sensing
FF	(none)	System Reset

MIDI uses a timebase of 24. That is, 24 times per beat (based on the tempo of the master instrument) a MIDI sequencer or drum machine will send out the code for synchronization called a *Timing Clock* through its MIDI OUT port. The code is F8 in hexadecimal, as shown in the chart above. The Timing Clock, like all Real Time messages, has no channel, as it is used to address all the instruments in a MIDI system. Instruments that do not use clocks, such as ordinary synthesizers, simply ignore the incoming clock data.

MIDI sequencers and drum machines run their clocks (even when they are not playing) to give any receiving machines a chance to calculate the tempo and synchronize from the very first beat of a song. Codes separate from the F8 Timing Clock are used for starting and stopping the music. MIDI *Start* is sent by the master to tell any other clock-based devices to start playing from the beginning of the song in their memory. They will play at the tempo being sent by the master. The *Stop* message is sent by the master to tell all the synchronized instruments to stop playing. *Continue* is used in a manner similar to Start. However, it signals the music to begin at whatever point it was last stopped.

As an example, look at a MIDI system with a sequencer as the master and a drum machine as the slave. The MIDI OUT jack from the sequencer is connected to the MIDI IN jack of the drum machine with a standard MIDI cable. In the sequencer's memory is MIDI data that has been recorded from a synthesizer. The drum machine's memory contains a rhythm part intended to go along with the music in the sequencer. This is a typical MIDI system setup:

Figure 10-3

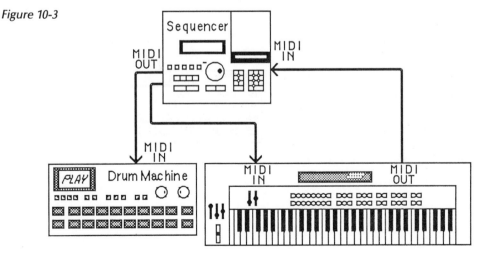

All MIDI sequencers and drum machines will have a synchronization option. This will include selecting *internal* or *external* sync. *Internal sync* turns a device into a master, using its own clock to determine the tempo. In the *external sync* mode (called *MIDI sync* on some instruments), an instrument uses the Timing Clocks from the master to determine its tempo. With the example above, the sequencer is in internal sync mode and the drum machine is set to external sync.

Even while the machines are not playing, the master is sending out Timing Clocks, preparing the slave to begin at the correct tempo. When the START button on the sequencer is pressed, a MIDI Start byte is sent along with the Timing Clocks to signal the drum machine to begin at the same time. The two machines run in exact synchronization. When STOP is pressed on the sequencer, both units will cease playing. Pressing CONTINUE on the sequencer will cause both units to start from the point at which they were stopped; pressing START will cause both machines to start from the first measure of the song.

If the preceding example of using MIDI Real Time with a sequencer and drum machine seems rather simple, that's because it is. The basic idea to remember in any MIDI system is to designate one clock-based device as the master, and use all the rest as slaves. Real Time messages are sent along with all the other MIDI messages, so it is possible to use the MIDI THRU jack of a synthesizer to connect a drum machine if your sequencer has only one MIDI OUT jack.

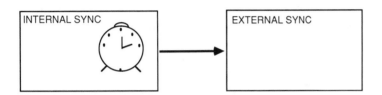

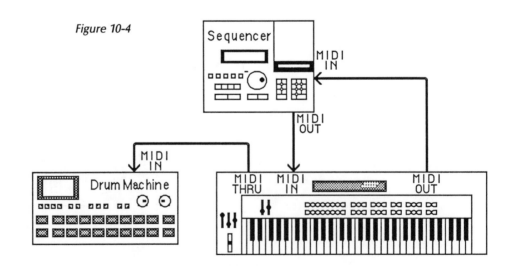

Figure 10-4

Active Sensing

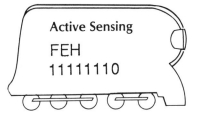

Active Sensing
FEH
11111110

What would happen if a MIDI cable were unplugged while a song was playing? While there is no harm done to instruments by plugging and unplugging MIDI cables with the power on, there would be a rather disastrous effect on the music. Any notes that were pressed down when the cable was removed would sustain indefinitely on the instrument connected to the controller. Any slaved rhythm machines that were playing at the time would grind to a halt.

Because MIDI only travels in one direction in a MIDI cable, a transmitting instrument is never aware of whether its signal is being received or not by another instrument. A function called *Active Sensing* has been implemented on some instruments to ensure that there will be no "hanging" notes or other problems in the event of a loss of connection. The Active Sensing message, FEH, is sent about three times every second (every 300 milliseconds to be exact). Once an instrument begins to receive Active Sensing, it will expect to continue receiving it. If there are no Active Sensing messages received after some period of time, the instrument will assume that there is a problem (maybe someone tripped over the cable). In this event, the instrument will simply shut down, turning off all notes that it is playing at the time. This is very useful for onstage performing, where accidents can happen at the most embarrassing times (such as when there are people in the audience).

Active sensing ensures that notes won't stick in the event that someone accidentally kicks out the MIDI plug.

System Reset

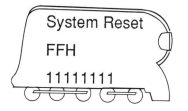

In the manual of practically every MIDI instrument is a description of how the instrument behaves when it is first turned on. Some instruments will be in Omni On/Poly while others will be Omni Off/Poly. Some instruments can be set to ignore or recognize velocity, aftertouch, or other MIDI controllers. Many of these parameters can be changed through MIDI or from the front panel so the instrument will function quite differently. The *System Reset* message is a command to tell a receiving instrument to go back to the mode it was in when first turned on. This message has no MIDI channel, so it will affect *all* the instruments connected to the sender. It is included as a Real Time message because it is usually sent only by sequencers, not synthesizers.

MTC (MIDI Time Code)

Synthesizers are being used more frequently in film and video production as both musical instruments and sound-effects generators. Low-cost digital *samplers* (instruments that can record natural acoustic sounds and then play them back musically from a keyboard) are giving sound designers a new palette of tone colors with which to work. The use of sound synthesis in film and video production has created a new set of needs for synchronization. In the case of sound effects, a sound must be triggered at just the right moment to match the picture. When a section of music, called a *cue*, is written for a film, it also must begin and end at specific points in the scene. MIDI Real Time messages are used for coordinating the performance of several instruments, ensuring that they run at the same tempo and are synchronized. However, the standard Real Time messages are not enough to handle all these special needs. While Real Time messages are *tempo-oriented,* film and video are *event-oriented.*

MTC, or *MIDI Time Code,* was added to MIDI to link the standard of the music world to *SMPTE Time Code,* the standard of the film and video world. SMPTE stands for "Society of Motion Picture and Television Engineers." It is the organization that developed the techniques used for film and video synchronization. SMPTE Time Code does not have tempo values associated with it. Instead it uses a clock that is calibrated very accurately in hours, minutes, seconds, and *frames* (of film or video). There are thirty frames per second in standard SMPTE Time Code. MTC works in conjunction with special hardware to read the SMPTE code from an audio or video tape. As the SMPTE time code is read from the tape, the MTC device sends the current hour, minute, second, and frame in MIDI format to a MIDI sequencer or computer program designed to read the MTC messages.

The basic MTC message, indicating the current position of the film or video, is sent four times every frame (120 times per second) in the following format:

Figure 10-5

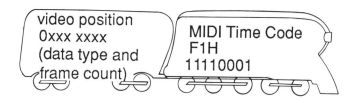

Events such as triggering individual notes in a synthesizer or sampler, starting or stopping a sequencer or drum machine, or even adjusting lights or cameras can be activated using a special *MIDI System Exclusive* code designed for use with MTC. An *event list* can be generated and sent from one MTC device to another, indicating when events will happen and what the events will be. When an event is about to happen, another System Exclusive message is sent by MTC devices to signal that it is time to trigger the next event in the list. The basic F1H message is sent in between events to keep all the MTC devices synchronized and ready.

While special MTC hardware exists, computers with MIDI interfaces are the primary tools for use with MTC. MTC is not usually transmitted in the same part of a MIDI system as Channel Messages. Here is a basic MTC setup:

Figure 10-6

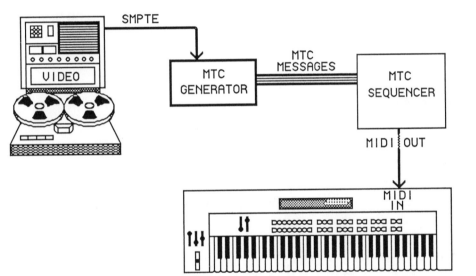

Chapter 11

System Common Messages

There are a small number of codes that are used to support other MIDI functions. These codes are called *System Common Messages.* Seven code numbers have been set aside for these messages, though not all are in use. These codes increase the power and usefulness of music systems that include sequencers, drum machines, or computers.

Song Position Pointer

Figure 11-1

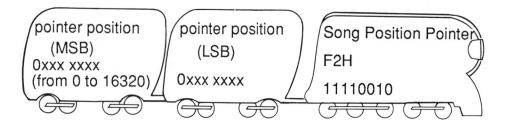

pointer position (MSB)
0xxx xxxx
(from 0 to 16320)

pointer position (LSB)
0xxx xxxx

Song Position Pointer
F2H
11110010

When a *Start* command is sent through MIDI, all clock-based instruments start playing from the beginning of the song programmed in their memory. If they are sent a *Stop* while playing, they will cease playing, hold their place in the music, and will play from that point if sent the *Continue* command.

Professional multitrack tape recorders have the ability to find specific points on a tape and play them. This function — *autolocating* — makes it much easier to fix or add something to the middle of a recording. You certainly wouldn't want to start at the beginning of a long song each time you wanted to hear the ending. Most MIDI sequencers and drum machines also have the ability to do some sort of *autolocating* by starting from a position other than the first measure of a song. It certainly adds to the strength of a MIDI recording system, and saves a lot of time.

However, let's assume you don't have any form of autolocating, you have a drum machine connected to your sequencer, and you wish to play from bar 32. You would need to set the bar number on the sequencer, set the bar number on the drum machine, put the drum machine into MIDI sync mode, and *then* press Start on the sequencer. You would need to do this every time you wanted to hear that section of the music.

Fortunately, MIDI can take care of this little chore for you with its *Song Position Pointer* command. Song Position Pointer is used in conjunction with System Real Time messages, the ones that link and synchronize the clocks in drum machines and sequencers into a system. It works like a MIDI autolocator. When a sequencer or drum machine is set to play from a certain measure, it will send this information out so that other clocked devices can also move to that same measure. When the machines are started by pressing Start on the master, a MIDI Continue message is sent and everything will begin from that point.

When a location is set on a sequencer or drum machine and the Song Position Pointer message is sent out, what is actually sent is the *number of sixteenth notes from the start of the piece* to the desired location. For example, if you set a sequencer to begin at bar 6 of a piece of music in 4/4 time, the sequencer will then send the Song Position Pointer out with the value 80, which is 20 x 4 (20 beats up to the beginning of the 6th bar times 4 sixteenths per beat).

Any other sequencer or drum machine that is connected to the master and is set to MIDI sync mode will respond by moving up in its own memory to the same location. When Start is pressed on the master, every machine will start from the same place. Not all sequencers or drum machines have Song Position Pointer implemented, but many do.

Song Select

Figure 11-2

Another handy ability to have is a master sequencer or drum machine that can tell other slaved devices which song to play — that is *Song Select*. Most drum machines and some sequencers can hold more than one song in their memory at one time. Songs are recalled by pressing a button on the machine's front panel. If you are performing on stage with sequencers and drum machines, it is useful to be able to select a song on just one machine and have all the others go to the same song.

Photo: Juke Boxes 4 Rent L.A.

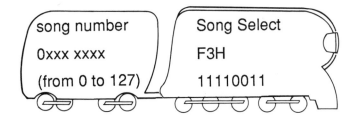

Obviously, a drum machine does not know which song is in which location of its internal memory. Song Select is just like Program Change in that the only thing sent is a number of a memory location. Whatever is in that location will play when Start is sent. It is your responsibility to be sure that Song #1 is the same in each machine.

Tune Request

End Of System Exclusive Flag

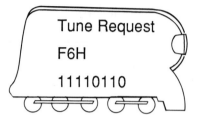

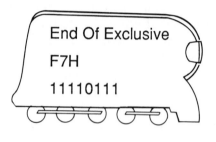

A problem shared by many analog synthesizers is that they can go out of tune over a short period of time. This is easily remedied on more modern synthesizers by the inclusion of a Tune button on the instrument. By pressing the button, a computer in the instrument will retune each oscillator (the actual sound-producing hardware) so it is in perfect tune with the others.

Analog MIDI synthesizers can be commanded to retune their oscillators by sending the System Common message *Tune Request.* It accomplishes the same task as pushing the Tune button on the instrument. This command is useful if, for example, a Tune Request is put into a sequencer during a moment of rest so an analog synthesizer can retune during that time. By their nature, digital synthesizers do not need, and will not respond to, Tune Request.

The final System Common message is the *End Of System Exclusive* message. This tells all receiving instruments that a System Exclusive message, such as a memory dump from a synthesizer or sampler, is finished. For more details see Chapter 12 on System Exclusive and its use.

What's Left

The other System Common codes — F4H and F5H — are still undefined. In general, System Common codes are used to augment other types of messages, and are not complete by themselves. See the chapters on Real Time and System Exclusive to have a better understanding of how the codes described above improve MIDI overall.

The Mysteries of System Exclusive

For the most part, MIDI communicates information that is common among electronic musical instruments. Regardless of what an instrument's method of producing sound (analog, digital, sampling, or a hybrid), most polyphonic MIDI instruments can exchange MIDI data about notes being played, pitch bending, modulation wheels, pedals, program changes, key velocity, and so forth. Sequencers and drum machines can share information about tempo, when to start and stop, and in some cases where to begin in a song.

System Exclusive messages are used for exchanging information that is *unique* to an instrument. The exchange is performed between two of the same instrument, or between an instrument and a computer. System Exclusive messages can be used for many possible applications, including:

1. Sending patch data from one instrument to another.

2. Transmitting the patterns from one drum machine to another.

3. Dumping the memory of a digital sampler to a computer for editing.

4. Sending song data from a sequencer to another sequencer or computer for backup.

5. Sending information about how the front panel of an instrument is being manipulated for use as a remote control for another instrument.

When a program or patch button is pressed on a synthesizer to call up another preset, *MIDI Program Change sends only the number of the memory location, not the data of the patch itself.* System Exclusive is used to send the actual data of a patch. Another synthesizer of the same make and model can receive the data and store it in its memory. The receiving instrument now has the same patch information and will produce the same sound.

Figure 12-1

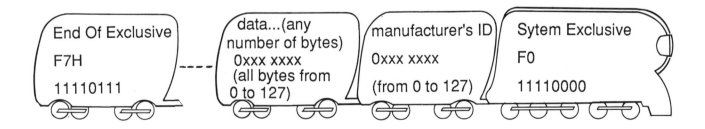

End Of Exclusive	data...(any number of bytes)	manufacturer's ID	Sytem Exclusive
F7H	0xxx xxxx	0xxx xxxx	F0
11110111	(all bytes from 0 to 127)	(from 0 to 127)	11110000

The figure above shows the format of a System Exclusive message. The first byte is the Status byte for System Exclusive. The second byte is a *Manufacturer's Identification* number. When a company designs MIDI instruments, they are given an ID number for all of their products by an official MIDI organization. In Japan, the organization is the Japanese MIDI Standards Committee (JMSC), and in the rest of the world it is the MIDI Manufacturers Association (MMA). The same ID number is used for all the products that will implement System Exclusive. A company has complete control over the format of any System Exclusive messages using that ID number. Other companies may create a product that is compatible with another company's Exclusive codes, if they wish, but they may not change anything about it.

There is no MIDI channel in the System Exclusive byte itself. When a receiver gets a "Start of Exclusive" byte, it waits for the ID byte to follow. If the ID number is from a different company, it will ignore all the data until the "End Of Exclusive" byte is received. After the manufacturer's ID, the format of the information is left up to the designer.

Usually, there is information immediately following the ID number to indicate the type of instrument and the MIDI channel of the sender. After that, the actual data is sent. A System Exclusive message always concludes with the "End Of Exclusive" byte (F0 in hexadecimal).

There is no predetermined number of data bytes in a System Exclusive message. There will be as many bytes as are needed to send the information along. A typical single patch may be anywhere from a few dozen to over a hundred bytes of data. Many instruments have a *bulk dump* function that will send the entire contents of their memories over MIDI to another instrument of the same type. A bulk dump may be hundreds or even thousands of bytes long.

Many MIDI instruments use System Exclusive messages to indicate that buttons or knobs on the front panel are being used. A short code is sent that indicates which knob is being used and what is being done to it. Here is an example:

Figure 12-2

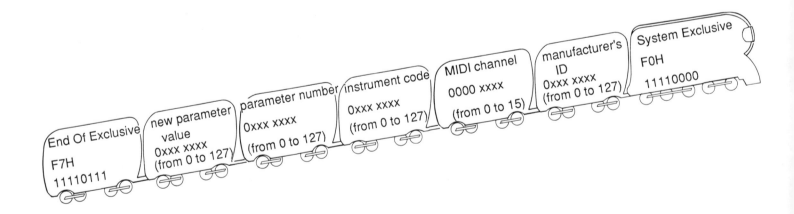

By sending information over MIDI that indicates how the front panel of a synthesizer is being manipulated, it is possible to use one instrument as a programming remote control for another. This is useful for creating or modifying patches in a rack-mounted MIDI sound module that may not have front panel knobs.

Figure 12-3

MIDI And The Personal Computer

Personal computers (PCs) have found a home with MIDI. While they can be very useful as sequencers, they are often indispensable as sound programmers, organizers, editors, and archives. With the proper software and MIDI interface, a PC becomes one of the most useful "instruments" in a MIDI system.

Aside from sequencing and educational software, there are two basic types of computer programs for use with MIDI instruments: *patch editors* and *patch librarians*. A patch editor is used for creating and modifying programs (patches) in a synthesizer. A patch librarian is for rearranging and organizing patches within an instrument or instruments. Both types of programs can exist only because of MIDI System Exclusive.

A typical PC setup includes MIDI software that is designed for that computer, a MIDI interface to allow MIDI information to be transferred into and out of the PC, MIDI cables going to and from the computer, and one or more synthesizers:

Figure 12-4

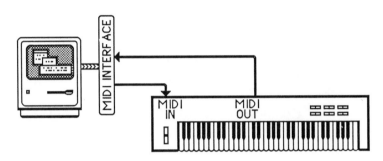

Because of the graphics capability, the large memory capacity, and the ability to load and save information on disk, the computer is a perfect partner in the MIDI world. Instruments with System Exclusive implementation can often be "requested" to send a copy of their memory out their MIDI OUT port. This request is in the form of a short System Exclusive message that is sent from the computer to the instrument. It can also be sent from another of the same instrument so they can share sounds. Upon receiving the request, the instrument will send out the patch data in its memory (many instruments also have the ability to send or receive a single patch as well). Instruments that do not respond to such a request via MIDI can usually send their data when a "bulk dump" button on their front panel is pressed.

Upon receiving a bulk dump, a computer can manipulate it in one of several ways:

• Store it, as is, for later retrieval.

• Display it on the screen for modification of the sound.

• Rearrange the order of the patches to better suit your needs.

• Take several "banks" of sounds and switch programs between them, as long as they are for the same model instrument.

Sample Dump Standard

A *sampler* is a musical instrument that produces a sound by digitally recording an acoustic sound and then playing it back from a keyboard or in response to MIDI messages. It consists of a device called an *analog-to-digital converter* (ADC) that converts sound into bytes, a very large amount of computer memory, and a device called a *digital-to-analog converter* (DAC) to convert the bytes back into sounds. By playing different keys on a sampler, the sounds are speeded up or slowed down which changes their pitch, thereby creating scales, chords, etc.

Computer software designed to manipulate samples via MIDI exists for several brands of computers and samplers. A copy of the sampler's memory is sent out in a long System Exclusive message through MIDI to the computer. The computer program can visually display the *waveforms* of the sound on its screen and allow them to be manipulated. The waveforms can then be saved to disk or returned to the sampler to be heard.

For the first few years of MIDI-controlled samplers, the format in which the samples were

transmitted via MIDI was different for each instrument. There was no standard way of sending and receiving sound through MIDI. Finally, in January of 1986, a standard for sample dumps was adopted by the worldwide organizations that govern the development of MIDI. The *Sample Dump Standard,* as it is called, is a universal System Exclusive format for sending and receiving samples through MIDI. Sounds can be sent from one sampler to another, or from a sampler to a personal computer.

The Sample Dump Standard consists of a *dump header,* a *data packet,* and five messages called *handshakes.* A handshake is a short message a receiving instrument sends to the sender to tell it that the data has been received correctly, that it has not been received correctly and please send it again, to wait before sending any more data, or that something isn't going right and please stop. Handshakes allow the communication to go both ways. In most MIDI systems, data is transmitted in one direction only, and the sender has no way of knowing if its data is being received or being received properly.

Using the MIDI Sample Dump Standard, the first action is a *Dump Request,* which is sent from

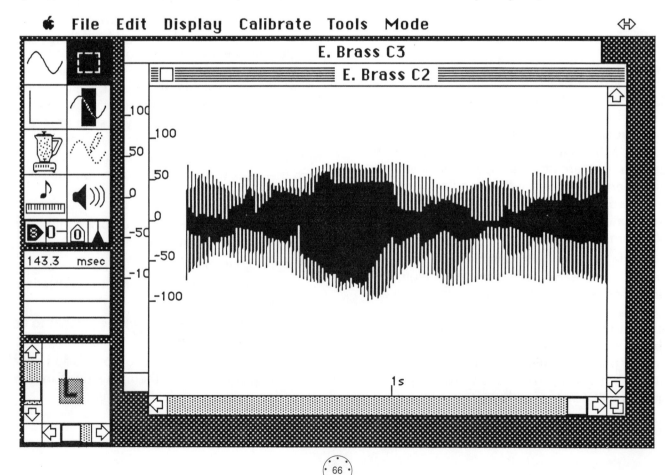

the computer or receiving instrument. The Dump Request is a short, 7-byte System Exclusive message. Upon receiving this request, a sampler that supports the Sample Dump Standard and is set to the same MIDI channel will send a Dump Header. A Dump Header is an exclusive message with information about the sample it will send, such as the size of the sample and the sampling rate at which it was recorded. If all is well, the receiver will send a handshake to continue, and the sampler will begin to send the memory dump in small chunks called *Data Packets.* The Data Packets are also System Exclusive messages with 120 bytes of the sampler's memory. There are tens or hundreds of thousands of bytes of data in a typical sample, so this usually takes several seconds to do. The Sample Dump Standard has not been implemented on all samplers.

Using System Exclusive

The need for using System Exclusive will come up only when you wish to send program data from one instrument to another, or to a computer for storage or manipulation. The techniques for doing this are different for each MIDI instrument, so you must consult the manual. Many instruments have a special mode for transmitting System Exclusive messages.

If you are working with a sequencer that is able to record System Exclusive messages along with other MIDI data, you may wish to enable your instruments to send System Exclusive, if possible. By doing this, any program changes made while recording the piece will record not only the program number, but the data of the patch itself. By following this procedure, it is not important to remember what patches were loaded in the synthesizer when the music was recorded. As the sequence plays back, the original sounds used during the recording will be retrieved and played.

System Exclusive is designed differently on each synthesizer. What its functions and capabilities are will also be different. If you are planning to use a personal computer for storing patches from your instruments, the software you purchase will give careful instructions of how to set up and use each instrument's System Exclusive capabilities.

Personal computers are powerful and easy to use.

Chapter 13

Putting It All Together

I t's finally time to look at what makes up a MIDI *system.* With an understanding of the INs, OUTs, and THRUs of MIDI, everything in this chapter should come together for you.

A MIDI system consists of one or more MIDI instruments, such as synthesizers, and MIDI cables. Options that can be added to a system are drum machines, sequencers, MIDI patch bays, synchronizers, computers and software, audio com-ponents (such as mixers, amps, tape machines, etc.), MIDI processors (such as channelizers, mergers, splitters, etc.), and one or more people — including yourself — to play and listen to the end result.

A MIDI system can be as simple as two instruments connected together with a single MIDI cable:

Figure 13-1

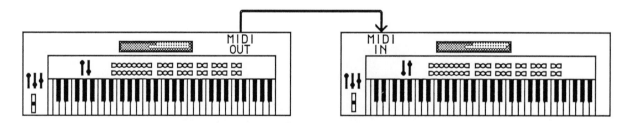

In this setup, playing on the master keyboard will play both instruments as long as they are set to the same MIDI channel.

The next level of sophistication would be to add a third instrument. This can be done either by using the MIDI THRU of the first slave, or by using a splitter box (also called a "THRU box") with one MIDI IN and several MIDI THRUs.

Figure 13-2

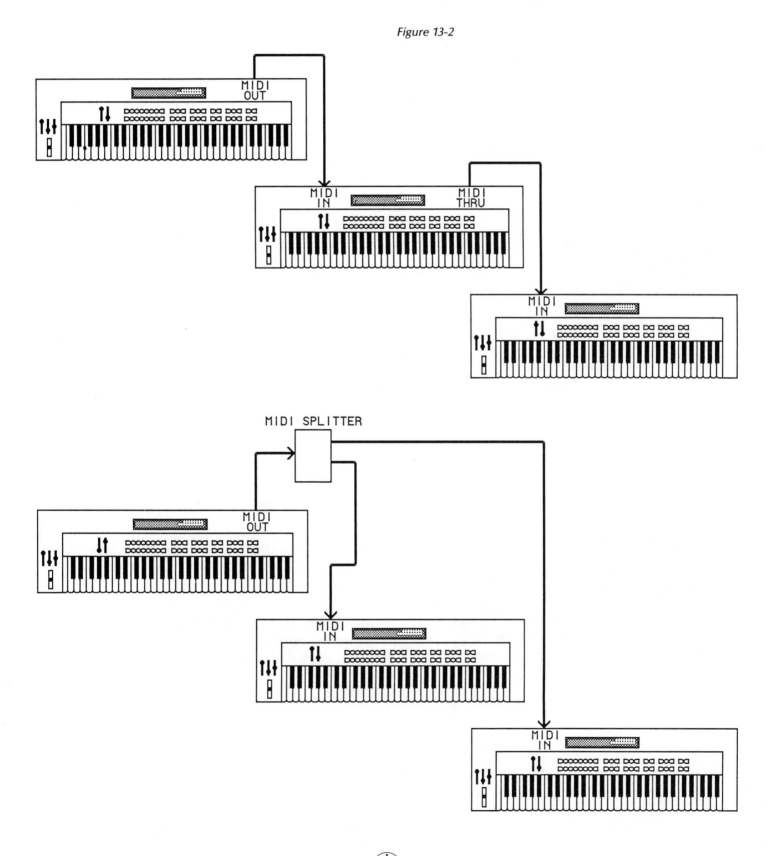

While both systems will work, there is a reason to use the setup with the splitter. First, using a splitter makes it possible to add even more instruments without building a long chain. It is always a good idea to look ahead. Using MIDI THRU once or twice will not produce problems. But problems can arise when "daisy chaining" a larger number of instruments.

Figure 13-3

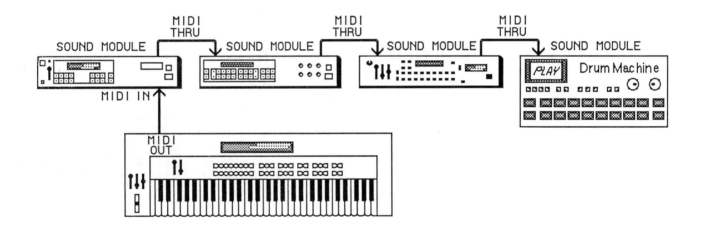

Each MIDI THRU jack has a small circuit to pass the MIDI signal on to the next instrument. This is helpful to facilitate sending MIDI over greater distances. However, each circuit can add a small amount of distortion to the MIDI signal, so that after a few generations of MIDI IN to MIDI THRU, the signal can get slightly damaged.

Depending on the circumstances, the distortion can be enough to create noticeable errors in the MIDI messages.

By using inexpensive splitters, not only is the possibility of errors and delays mostly removed, but setting up, adding to, and reconfiguring a MIDI system is easier.

The next item that is usually added to a growing MIDI system is a drum machine. Initially you don't need MIDI to play a keyboard and use a drum machine that has a song programmed in it. In most cases you simply start the machine and play along. However, MIDI can still be used for playing multiple synths. When a sequencer is added, the MIDI IN jack of a drum machine becomes much more important as you will see shortly.

For now, take a look at the ways to connect a sequencer with one or more MIDI instruments.

Figure 13-4

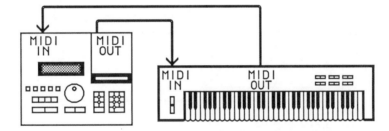

• Two MIDI cables are used to connect a MIDI keyboard with a MIDI sequencer.

• The MIDI OUT of the synthesizer goes to the MIDI IN of the sequencer so data can be sent to it.

• The sequencer will be sending data back to the synthesizer upon playback, so a second cable is used to connect the sequencer's MIDI OUT back to the instrument's MIDI IN.

• With this system it is possible to record, play and overdub, if the sequencer is capable of it.

Adding one or more instruments to the setup above adds immensely to the power of the system. One instrument functions as the master, while all the instruments will function as slaves to the sequencer. This is how such a setup could look:

Figure 13-5

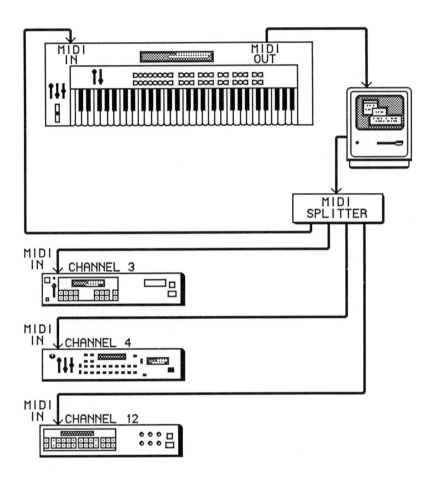

• The MIDI OUT of the master keyboard is used to send MIDI data to the sequencer.

• The output of the sequencer is then connected to a splitter and sent to all the synthesizers in the system including the master.

• Each synthesizer is set to a different MIDI channel.

• By changing the MIDI channel on the master, different instruments in the system can be selected.

• The sequencer will remember the channel assignments as it records the data so on playback each instrument can be playing a different individual part.

With the addition of a sequencer, a drum machine is probably not far behind (unless you are far behind on the payments for your sequencer). The setup will look something like Figure 13-6:

Figure 13-6

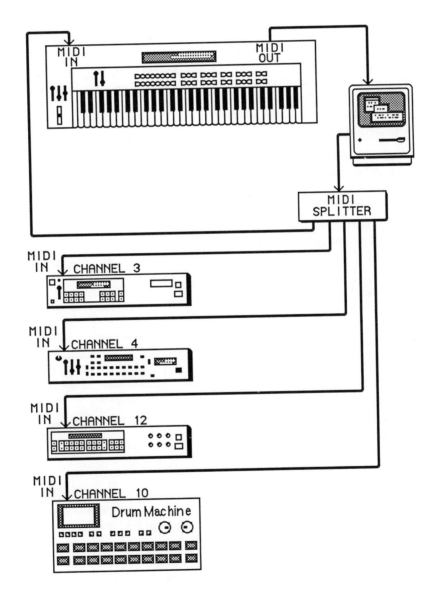

MIDI drum machines can work in one of two ways with a sequencer: as a clock-based slave, or as a sound module. In the first case, the following points must be considered:

- MIDI sequencers transmit MIDI Clocks based on their internal tempo setting.

- The drum machines, which are connected to the MIDI OUT of the sequencer, will synchronize their performances to those clocks and lock with the sequencer when it is started.

- It is important that the drum machine is set to MIDI Sync Mode, as opposed to Internal Sync Mode.

- Once the machines are connected and set to the proper modes, the sequencer will run the drum machine, making it unnecessary to touch the drum machine to start or stop it.

Most MIDI drum machines also have the ability to act as a sound module by responding to Note On information from an external source: Drum parts can be played from a MIDI keyboard, recorded into a MIDI sequencer, and played back on the drum machine. The advantage of this is that the drum parts are recorded and stored along with the rest of the music in the sequencer's memory. In this situation, the drum machine is not put into MIDI Sync Mode, since it is not using the sequencer's clock. The drum machine is being used only as a MIDI sound module.

A MIDI drum machine assigns a certain MIDI key number or numbers to each of its internal drum sounds. By hitting the proper key on the MIDI keyboard, the corresponding drum will sound. A look in the owner's manual of a MIDI drum machine will show you how to assign the drum sounds to key numbers and how to change them to suit your own tastes and needs. By playing drums into a sequencer from a MIDI keyboard, you are saving the drum parts along with the rest of the song.

In designing your own music system, you must also consider the audio output of the instruments. The MIDI connections shown above make no contribution to the audio portion of a music system. For each audio output of an instrument, you will need to have an input on an amplifier or mixer. Many instruments have stereo outputs, and

drum machines often have a separate output for each individual drum sound. It becomes clear that a MIDI system of any size or complexity won't fly without adequate audio capabilities. Fortunately, this need not be expensive with the availability of smaller *keyboard mixers* or even one of the small four-track cassette "studios" that often have four-track or six-track mixers built into them.

Tape Synchronization

One of the goals of putting together a more advanced MIDI system is not only to play and sequence, but to record your music on audio tape as well. This brings up the need to synchronize the sequencer to a multitrack tape machine, which can be done in different ways: most sequencers and drum machines have some form of built-in *sync to tape.* Tape sync is a special type of audio signal that is recorded onto one track of the tape and then played back into the sequencer. It's simple to use. The sequencer or drum machine uses this signal to lock itself to the tape as it is playing or recording:

Figure 13-7

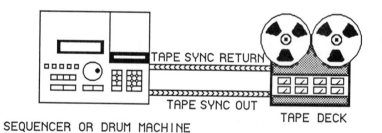

TAPE SYNC RETURN

TAPE SYNC OUT

SEQUENCER OR DRUM MACHINE

TAPE DECK

All sequencers and drum machines have clocks inside them to control tempo. A tape sync signal uses this clock and converts it into tones that are recordable on tape. The digital clock signal (marked *clock out* on most machines) used for synchronizing certain devices can not be recorded on tape. The tape sync signal created by a sequencer, called an FSK signal (Frequency-Shifted Key), reflects the tempo at which the machine is running. When the FSK tone is played back into a sequencer or drum machine that is set to Tape Sync Mode, the tone is used as the master clock. Since tape speeds fluctuate slightly, so will the sync tone being sent back to the sequencer. In turn, the sequencer, which is using the tone as its own clock, also adjusts to keep pace with the tape. As each track is recorded on the tape, the same pattern occurs, the end result being that each track of the tape is perfectly synchronized to the others.

Using a mutitrack recorder, even a simple four-track cassette studio, gives more power to any MIDI system. Being able to synchronize and overdub tracks on tape gives the effect of having many more instruments. If there are more parts in your music than there are instruments available, a few parts can be recorded at a time on each track of the tape machine. If you want to get a special sound that is only possible by layering two or more instruments, this is possible too.

One way to use tape in a multi-instrument MIDI sequencer system is to record all the parts first into the sequencer without using the tape. After all the parts are entered and edited in the sequencer, they can then be recorded by playing a few of the sequenced parts at a time onto each track of the tape machine.

Another approach is to sequence some parts of the music and then record them to tape before continuing on to more parts of the song. With this technique, instruments can play new parts since the first parts are on the tape and don't need to be in the sequence any longer. With most sequencers that have a tape sync function it is possible to record as well as play in tape sync mode. This means that you can be listening to a tape playback while recording into the sequencer and all the parts with be synchronized. Then, after any fixing or editing in the sequencer, the new parts can be laid to tape using any available synthesizers.

Tape synchronization is not available on every sequencer or drum machine. When it is not, it is necessary to add a synchronizer to the system that will link the tape machine to the sequencer. Most companies use the FSK technique described above. Others use a click that is recorded to tape and is converted to either a clock signal or directly to MIDI Real Time messages when played back into the machine.

SMPTE-MIDI, Film, and Video

Another, more sophisticated technique for synchronization is the use of SMPTE time code. SMPTE is a timing system that was originally developed for the synchronization of film, video and audio devices. It is extremely accurate and is most useful for anyone producing music for film or video. A SMPTE time code "stripe" is recorded on tape in much the same way that FSK would be. A synchronizer is used to link the SMPTE track (which can be recorded on one track of a multi-track tape or can be on a video tape) to the MIDI system. An advantage of using SMPTE is that the tempo of the music is not recorded to the sync track as it is with FSK or click. SMPTE records *real time* onto the track. Time is divided into hours, minutes, seconds, frames, and bits. There are usually thirty frames in a second and eighty bits in a frame. This provides a timing accuracy of .0004 of a second.

A device that converts SMPTE into MIDI synchronization has the ability to read the SMPTE time code and store a specific tempo (or tempos) into its memory. When SMPTE is received, the device locks onto the time and knows the exact time to send each clock pulse out through MIDI. In this type of sync system, not only is the tempo remarkably accurate and flexible, but it's adjustable in very small increments. Beats can be moved forward or backward to align with a frame of film or video. In a multitrack recording, an overdubbed part that feels early or late can be adjusted to match the rest of the tracks by telling the SMPTE-to-MIDI converter to begin a frame or two earlier or later. Since SMPTE time code does not contain tempo, it is possible to record a sync stripe onto tape and change your mind about tempo later. This is impossible to do with an FSK or click track.

There are currently several devices for recording and reading SMPTE and converting to MIDI Real Time code that allow tempos to be entered and recorded, and lock the tempo to a SMPTE stripe. They each have "audio in" and "out" to connect to a tape machine or video recorder, as well as MIDI OUT to connect to a sequencer or drum machine. The connection is the same as Figure 13-7. A MIDI IN jack is also provided on these devices to let a master keyboard (the one used for recording the sequences) record into the sequencer along with the clock of the synchronizer. The MIDI data from the keyboard is blended with the MIDI clock pulses from the synchronizing device and the mixed signal is sent on to the sequencer.

Figure 13-8

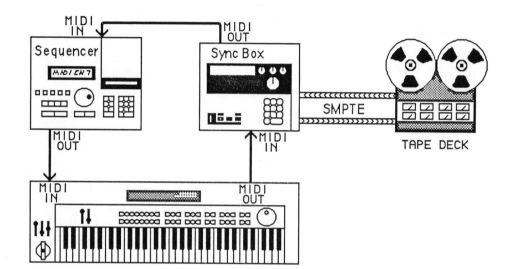

Surprises are not always desired when putting your studio together.

The Dreaded MIDI Feedback

A situation may arise in which you will want to connect two sequencers to transfer data from one to the other. (Perhaps to give a song to a friend or to use a sequencer with some editing ability that yours does not have.) The setup for this is simple: If data is being moved in just one direction, simply take the MIDI OUT of the sequencer *with* the data and connect it to the MIDI IN of the sequencer that's to *receive* the data. Put the receiving sequencer into "MIDI sync mode" and "record mode" simultaneously, and then press PLAY on the master.

With the two units in sync, it doesn't matter at what tempo you are transferring the data. You can even play back the song at a very high speed to reduce the transfer time.

However, a given sequencer may not work well recording in MIDI sync mode, in which case it should serve as the master. The sequencer that is sending the data should become the slave unit by going into its MIDI sync mode. To do this, *both* MIDI INs and OUTs must be connected on the two units. One cable to send the data, the other to handle the sync functions.

Sequencers, unlike synthesizers, will usually echo the data arriving at the MIDI IN jack directly to the MIDI OUT, performing the same function as a MIDI THRU on a synthesizer. This is done in order to merge the data being played by the sequencer with any data that is coming into the sequencer during an overdub. There is usually a switch on the sequencer to defeat the merging function, which is sometimes called *echo, thru, mix,* or *soft-thru.* If both sequencers are echoing their MIDI IN to their MIDI OUT, a dreaded feedback loop will occur!

MIDI data being played by the first sequencer will be echoed by the receiver which passes it back to the master which echoes it again. To prevent this, you need to be sure that at least one of the sequencers has its *thru* function turned off.

"An Early Example Of MIDI Feedback"

Figure 13-9 "Waterfall" by M.C. Escher (lithograph 1961) Figures of lithographs and woodcuts of M.C. Escher are reproduced by permission of the Escher Foundation, Haags

Gemeentemuseum, the Haag. Copyright © The Escher Foundation, 1979. Reproduction rights arranged courtesy of the Vorpal Galleries, New York and San Francisco.

MIDI Patch Bays

As the sophistication of music systems grows, the need for organizing the connection between various components becomes more and more important. Recording studios, for example, require an enormous amount of audio equipment, each piece having inputs and outputs. It is often necessary to change the way components are connected: The output of a tape track may need to go to a mixer at one point and to a delay device next. A microphone can be connected to an input channel of the mixer, to a compressor, or to a special effects device. This is called *patching.* As a musical situation changes, so does the patching of the system.

If you have just one or two MIDI instruments, or do not use sequencers or patch librarians, a MIDI patch bay is not of great importance. However, if you find yourself always changing cables around and reconfiguring your system to do different things, these devices are definitely time-savers. So, add a *MIDI patch bay* to the list of MIDI devices you might need.

A typical MIDI patch bay has several MIDI INs and MIDI OUTs. By using controls on the patch bay's front panel, it can route any IN to any OUT. A patch bay may also have some memory, so that system setups can be stored and then recalled at the touch of a button. Many patch bays will even respond to MIDI Program Change messages to move from one setup to another. Some patch bays are able to send two INs to the same OUT. Merging two MIDI data streams is technically difficult and usually out of the realm of an ordinary patch bay, though there are units that will accomplish this. However, an output can be connected to any one of the inputs. It is also possible to route one input go to several outputs in order to split the MIDI information and send it to several instruments at once.

MIDI patch bays are almost essential in a MIDI system with a patch librarian and a personal computer. A typical sequencer or computer MIDI interface has a single MIDI IN jack. That precious input is usually connected to the master keyboard of the system. If you wish to do a System Exclusive data dump from another instrument into the sequencer or special patch library program, it may be necessary to unplug the keyboard and connect the other instrument. Then, when you are done, you must put everything back. A patch bay solves this problem by allowing you to choose the way that all the MIDI cables will be connected for a given application. For instance, you may have a setup for sequencing, another for dumping System Exclusive data from different instruments into the computer or sequencer, and yet another for using a computer to program sounds on different instruments or sound modules.

Figure 13-10 A J.L. Cooper MIDI Patch Bay

The Never-Ending Story

There is no end to the devices, instruments, controllers, processors and synchronizers that can be added to a MIDI-based music system. Putting together a good MIDI system means deciding just what your needs are and designing the most flexible way to achieve them. With a bit of common sense, most MIDI systems should be relatively simple to design. The diagrams in this chapter are good examples of some of the ways in which a basic MIDI system is put together.

Putting It All Together For Yourself

To put together a diagram of your own system, or your planned system, get a pencil and paper and draw each component or module that you have or plan to get. Use the diagrams in this chapter as examples. Draw lines to connect each of the components one at a time:

• Begin with the MIDI OUT of the master instrument.

• From there go to the first destination.

• If there is a series of destinations, include a splitter or a patch bay depending on your needs.

• Remember that MIDI data going into an instrument comes out the MIDI THRU port, not the MIDI OUT. The exception to this general rule is found in sequencers and "mother" keyboards.

As you progress, the logic of MIDI data flow should become clearer and clearer. MIDI can be adapted to nearly any situation without the need for odd solutions. The best system for you is based on the the type of music you make, the equipment you have, and the way you feel most comfortable using it. If you plan to use your system for more than one function (sequencing and patch organization, for example), try making a separate diagram for each function. Look for common connections and see how they can be brought together into a MIDI system to handle all your musical needs.

The key to success in any craft is in knowing how to use the tools available.

Chapter 14

Buying MIDI Instruments

Here are some tips on what to look for when starting, or adding to, a MIDI music system.

1. Decide upon your needs and establish a budget. A MIDI system can be made up of MIDI instruments such as synthesizers, rhythm machines, and a sequencer, as well as a mixer, an amplifier, speakers, audio signal processors, a tape recorder, a synchronizer, and the cables to connect everything together. You will probably not need all of these devices (at least not at first), so it is important to know which you do need in order to produce the kind of music you want.

2. Buy a little at a time. Learn an instrument or two at a time before going on to the next one. If you are unhappy with an instrument, you may wish to return, exchange, or sell it before adding another one to your system.

3. Test each instrument you plan to buy to be sure it has the features you want. For instance, if you are a pianist, it might be important to have a sixteen-voice instrument instead of a six-voice or eight-voice one. Decide if velocity sensitivity is important to you. It adds greater expressive control, but it adds to the expense of an instrument. It is not always possible to return an expensive synthesizer. If you are a composer, it may be important for versatility to get an instrument capable of producing multiple timbres at one time. Most importantly, be sure you like the sound of the synthesizer or drum machine you are planning to buy. Different instruments use a variety of synthesis techniques and will sound different. They will not be able to mimic each other.

4. Look through the manual before buying. Unfortunately, not all owner's manuals are created equal, so be sure that you can get one that is concise and understandable. Check that the instrument does what you need it to do. If you're buying a sequencer, see that it has the features you consider important.

5. Ask a lot of questions at the store. Part of what you pay for when you purchase equipment is service and support from the store at which you are buying. The store personnel should be able to answer your questions or find the answers for you. After you have made a purchase, you should be able to call the salesperson from whom you made the purchase for any assistance.

6. Examine the MIDI implementation chart of the instrument in the manual. Every MIDI instrument comes with a guide that shows exactly what the instrument's MIDI capabilities are. The charts are in the same format for every instrument.

7. Test the instrument with your existing equipment (if possible). While it is rare, there are some instances when two instruments may not work well together. To be completely certain that your planned system will work, try using the components you have with the ones you wish to add — this includes sequencers.

8. If you have questions that neither the salesperson nor the manual can answer, have the store call the manufacturer. You deserve to have all your questions answered thoroughly. A salesperson at a store can't know every answer, but it is his or her responsibility to be certain that you get every question answered to your satisfaction. Don't hesitate to request that the manufacturer be called to confirm an "I think so" or "it should" by the salesperson.

9. Don't be reluctant to get a MIDI splitter or selector box if it will simplify your setup. As a MIDI system grows in size, using the MIDI THRUs provided in the instruments becomes less and less desirable, if even possible. A *MIDI splitter* or "thru box" is an inexpensive and efficient way to clean up the "mess" of MIDI cables. If you are using a patch librarian with a personal computer, you will need to select different instruments to be connected to the single MIDI IN of your computer interface. A *MIDI input selector,* or a *MIDI patch bay* will solve the problem of needing to change the MIDI connections in your system.

10. It's better to save a little longer and get the one thing you want, than to buy now and get three things you won't like. The best things in life may be free, but musical instruments can get a bit expensive. It is important to get the most for your money. While the points above are presented to help you make the best decisions, it also is worth mentioning that the instrument you really want may not be the cheapest one in the store (in fact, it rarely is). This may be especially true for the master controller of a system. Slave instruments are as good as they sound, but it is much more important for a master keyboard to feel good and act as a good controller for the rest of the system.

11. If you are buying MIDI software for your computer, check the following:
   a. ...Will it run on your computer? Not all "compatibles" will run software designed for a particular computer.
   b. ...Are you getting the right MIDI interface for your machine? Computers cannot automatically connect to MIDI, a special interface card is necessary (the Atari ST is an

Your "friendly" musical instrument store

exception). There are several interfaces on the market and they are not usually compatible with one another. Also, software will only work with the MIDI interface for which it was designed.

c. ...Does your computer have the necessary memory and peripherals for the software?

d. Test the program before you buy, or at least read the manual in its entirety. Most music stores have a "no return" policy for MIDI software.

e. If possible, test the program with the equipment you have. There are some cases in which a particular sequencer program does not work well with a particular brand of synthesizer.

f. If you require tape sync, be sure it is available on the system you are buying.

g. Check that the manufacturer has a reasonable policy for obtaining updates as they become available and for getting backup disks if the program is copy-protected (not copyable).

Buying the right equipment is a critical step towards having a good musical environment in which to work. The people at the store are, of course, there to sell equipment. By being demanding about information and service, you will have a better chance of getting the goods and services you desire. The purchase of a musical instrument does not begin and end with the item in the box. It includes a relationship with both the company that made it and the people who sold it to you.

Another way to insure that you are making the right choice is by talking to people who already own the equipment you are considering buying. Ask friends, or the store from which you will be buying, to put you in touch with an owner of that equipment. This can be very helpful for both hardware and software purchases.

Buying MIDI equipment should not be a shot in the dark, nor should it be a grueling experience leaving you with horror stories to tell friends. It should be a thoughtful, simple and fulfilling task that provides you with the tools you need to expand your creativity.

"It doesn't?!!...I should have read the manual before buying!"

Chapter 15

Problem Solving

Although MIDI is simple and straightforward, problems do occasionally come up. Not all MIDI instruments are perfect. There are some mistakes that have caused people to wonder if they are going crazy when something doesn't work the way they think it should. While it isn't possible to cover every problem that can occur when setting up and using a MIDI system, here are a few of the more common pitfalls and misunderstandings that happen with MIDI:

"I have connected two MIDI instruments, but when I play on the master, the other synth doesn't make a sound."

This could be due to one or a number of possible reasons:

1. The audio output of the receiver is not connected or is not on. Check the cables and the mixer or amplifier. Check the volume setting on the receiving instrument as well.

2. MIDI OUT of the master is not connected to MIDI IN on the receiver. Check the MIDI cables to be sure they are there and are connected to the right ports.

3. The receiver is set to a different MIDI channel than the master. Check both instruments to see that they are set to the same MIDI channel.

4. If the master is running through a sequencer before going to the receiver, the sequencer must be set to pass MIDI IN to MIDI OUT. This function goes by different names on different sequencers. It is called *echo, thru, mix, soft-thru, or patch thru.* In any case, this function must be set "On" in order for the data to pass to receiving instruments.

"I have one synthesizer and a sequencer. I recorded a bass part into my sequencer and then set the synthesizer to play a flute part for an overdub. When I played back the sequence, the bass part sounded terrible."

1. A sequencer has no way of knowing the sound a synthesizer is making when it is recording. *A MIDI sequencer does not record sound, only performance.* It is not possible to record another track on a sequencer with a second sound, unless the synthesizer has the ability to be split into two or more parts with different sound presets.

The first rule of MIDI is: *MIDI does not give an instrument any abilities it does not have to begin with.* In other words, if a synthesizer has eight voices, it will continue to have only eight voices. If it is not velocity sensitive, it will not become velocity sensitive. MIDI doesn't change the functions on an instrument, it simply allows the instrument to connect with other instruments. In this case, the problem is that a synthesizer capable of producing only one timbre at a time (as most are), will still not be able to produce more than one timbre at a time even when connected to a sequencer.

2. If an instrument can be split, then each part will most likely have its own MIDI channel. When doing an overdub, be sure to set the keyboard to send on the proper MIDI channel for the split.

"My drum machine doesn't start when my sequencer does."

1. Be sure that you have MIDI OUT of the sequencer going to MIDI IN of the drum machine.

2. Not all drum machines are MIDI compatible. If yours is not, then you must use some other form of synchronization, such as clock or tape sync. This will be different for different machines. If a drum machine does not have MIDI, and your sequencer does not have a CLOCK OUT facility, you will need a separate synchronizer with both MIDI and clock outputs to be the master clock for the entire system or a device able to convert MIDI into clock pulses.

3. With a MIDI drum machine, be sure that it is set to play and is in MIDI Sync mode. This is set differently on different machines.

"When I play on the master everything plays, including the drums in the drum machine."

Many MIDI instruments are in Omni On mode when they first are turned on. This means that they will play everything, regardless of the MIDI channel to which they are set. The solution for this is contained in MIDI Rule Number Two: *Always turn on the receivers in a MIDI system before the masters.* When powering everything on, first turn the receiving instruments and drum machines on. Next, turn the sequencer on if one is in use. Then last, turn the master keyboard on. The reason for this is that many instruments, and nearly all sequencers, will automatically *send* an Omni Off message when they are first turned on. This message will ensure that the receivers are in the correct mode for sequencing.

"I have sequenced a few tracks and the parts are starting to sound funny; notes are very short and not the way I played them."

This goes back to Rule Number One: If an instrument is an eight-voice polyphonic synthesizer, it will not "grow" more voices when it is used with a sequencer. For instance, if you play a five-note chord and record that onto track one of a sequencer, and on track two you play another five-note chord simultaneously, upon playing the two tracks back there will be ten Note On messages sent to the synthesizer. The synthesizer will have to make a decision as to which notes to play with its eight voices, and which to ignore. The results are usually not too pleasing. When sequenc-

ing and doing overdubs for the same synthesizer, be sure not to go beyond the number of voices available in the instrument.

"I was changing MIDI channels from my main keyboard to listen to some other synths. As I was playing, notes would stick "on" sometimes, and I couldn't shut them off."

A note is made up of two separate MIDI *commands:* a Note On and a Note Off. When a key is pressed, the Note On is sent. If the MIDI channel is changed before the key is released, then the Note Off will be on a different MIDI channel, and will be ignored by the receiving synth. The same will be true of pedals, wheels, or any other controllers. Be sure to release the keys before changing the channel. If a note is stuck, press the same key again and hold it down. Then go back to the channel the receiving synth is on and release the key.

"My sequencer claims it can record 10,000 notes, but it seems to run out of memory much sooner than that. Was the company not telling the truth, or am I doing something wrong? Can I do something to increase its capacity?"

In MIDI, a note is made up of two separate events: a Note On and a Note Off. While it is very useful to know the note capacity of a sequencer, the number of notes may not be the best way to measure memory. It is better to say that a sequencer able to record 10,000 notes is capable of recording about 20,000 *MIDI events.*

Many MIDI keyboards put out other information in addition to Note Ons and Offs that can consume a lot of memory. One of the biggest memory users is aftertouch. Keyboards with aftertouch often generate these messages even if the aftertouch function is not turned on in the patch itself. In some cases, there is a separate switch to shut off the sending of aftertouch.

Pitch bend and modulation also can eat up a lot of memory space in a sequencer. If it is important to record a large number of notes in a sequence, be as sparing as possible with continuous controllers.

Conclusions

Now that you've gotten a glimpse into the internal workings of one of the great phenomenons of modern music, it might be worthwhile to look at the importance of all this information. Certainly a musician doesn't need to know how to build a synthesizer in order to play it. Why then is it important to understand so much about MIDI?

MIDI instruments, by their power and ease of use provide a source of great inspiration to musicians and composers. It was previously very difficult to move from sound to sound, especially sounds using more than one instrument. With the greater amount of ease that MIDI provides to trying out sounds or creating new ones by combining existing ones, musicians are much more likely to experiment. MIDI then is directly responsible for enhancing the creative possibilities of electronic instruments by making them easier to use.

Along with this simplicity also comes a new level of complexity, however. MIDI has given rise to the idea of a *personal music system,* with multiple instruments, sequencing, rhythm machines, tape sync, SMPTE, patch bays, etc. To design and use a personal music system to its maximum capability does indeed require a solid understanding of MIDI's INs, OUTs, and THRUs.

As an example, a sequencer with the capability of editing individual MIDI events can be frustrating or useless to the musician that doesn't have a firm grasp of what it is he or she is looking at. As a creative option, what if you wished to insert a pedal or MIDI volume message into a sequence. It is important to know what codes exist and what they are in order to use them.

MIDI is a tool. And like most any other tool, does not replace anything. It is important to keep a certain perspective in mind when buying or using MIDI equipment. That is that MIDI is just one tool. Technique, musicianship, and common sense are others that also go into making good music. If you are building a house you would use a hammer, but you won't built a house out of hammers. It's the same with MIDI. It is one tool to be mastered and used with the many others to build music that is expressive and professional.

Artistic freedom is within your grasp!

Glossary

Active Sensing: A MIDI message sent by some instruments that tells receiving instruments to shut off during performance in the event that a MIDI cable is disconnected.

Aftertouch: (Also called *"key pressure."*) A MIDI Continuous Controller code sent by some keyboards when pressure is applied to a key after it has been struck.

Amplitude: Volume.

Amplitude Modulation (AM): The periodic changing of amplitude (volume) to create expressive effects such as tremolo.

Analog: In synthesis, the use of voltages to control the pitch, timbre, and amplitude of a sound.

Baud Rate: Usually, the speed (in bits-per-second) at which data travels from device to device. For example, MIDI travels at 31,250 baud.

Binary: The number system used by computers to represent information. (Also called *"base 2."*) Numbers in the binary system can have a value of either 0 or 1.

Bit: A single binary digit stored in a computer device. Bits can have a value of either 0 or 1, forming what is called "binary code." (See *"Binary"*) MIDI sends bits from instrument to instrument in special code combinations.

Breath Controller: A MIDI Continuous Controller code generated by a device that is sensitive to air pressure. It is used by placing the device in the mouth and blowing. The breath controller is typically used to produce modulation.

Bulk Dump: In MIDI, the transmission of the entire contents of an instrument's memory via System Exclusive to another compatible instrument or to a computer.

Byte: A group of eight bits. Bits are arranged in groups of 8 to represent a larger range of numbers. MIDI messages are sent as a series of bytes.

Channel: An informational pathway over which MIDI data is transmitted or received. MIDI can transmit or receive information on as many as sixteen channels over a single MIDI cable. The lower four bits of each MIDI status byte indicate the MIDI channel for the data bytes that follow. (See Chapter 5)

Channel Key Pressure: A MIDI message sent when a key is pressed down after it has been struck. The value generated by the key that is pressed the hardest is used for the entire MIDI channel.

Channel Mode Messages: See *"Mode Messages"*

Channel Number: The lower four bits of each MIDI status byte which indicate the MIDI channel number for the data bytes that follow.

Channel Voice Messages: The MIDI codes that represent the actual musical performance. These include Note On and Off, Pitch Bend, Continuous Controllers, Program Changes, and Aftertouch.

Clock Rate: See *"Resolution"*

Code: A system of communication using special symbols to represent information. MIDI is a code.

Continue: The MIDI code that tells a sequencer or drum machine to play from the point at which it was last stopped.

Continuous Controllers: Any of the MIDI codes created by moving wheels, levers, pedals, or sliders. Modulation wheel and breath controller are examples of continuous controllers.

Control Change: The category of MIDI messages created by continuous controllers, switches or pedals.

Control Voltage: In analog synthesis, the technique of using voltages to represent and control the various parameters of a synthesizer.

Data: Information.

Data Bytes: The bytes sent after a MIDI status byte to define the specific values of information being sent.

Delay: (Also called a *"Digital Delay Line,"* or *"DDL."*) An audio effects device to produce echoes and reverberations.

Digital: The numerical representation of information. For example, MIDI uses numbers to represent performance information. Many synthesizers use numbers to create and represent waveforms. Sampling keyboards store sounds as numbers. Thus all these devices are considered *digital.*

DIN — Deutche Industrie-Norm: A standard type of electrical connector, developed in Germany.

Effects: Devices that change the characteristics of an audio signal passed through them. Reverb, delay, chorus, flanging, equalization, and panning units are all effects. Sometimes called *"signal processors."*

External Sync: In MIDI, the mode on a sequencer or drum machine in which the device uses incoming MIDI Timing Clocks to determine its tempo, as well as when it will start and stop playing.

Frequency Modulation (FM):   The periodic changing of frequency to create expressive effects such as vibrato. Frequency Modulation (FM) can also be used to synthesize entirely new sounds.

FSK — Frequency Shift Keying: A technique to record clock pulses onto audio tape by using different tones to represent the pulses. FSK is often used to synchronize sequencers and drum machines to tape.

Hexadecimal: (Also called *"hex."*) A method for representing numbers in base sixteen. Digits 0 to 9 are used along with letters A to F. Hexadecimal numbers are used to make MIDI information eas-ier to read, since there are sixteen unique hexadecimal digits to represent the sixteen MIDI channels in any status byte.

Hold: The MIDI code sent when a sustain pedal is pressed. It commands instruments to continue holding any notes that are currently being played even after a MIDI Note Off message has been received.

Interface: The interconnection of separate devices to create a larger system.

Internal Sync: The mode in which a sequencer or drum machine uses its own clock to determine tempo.

Key Number: A numerical value for each key of a keyboard. MIDI has 128 key numbers (0–127).

Key Pressure: See *"Aftertouch."*

LSB — Least Significant Byte: A second data byte, used for increasing the resolution of some MIDI controllers.

Manufacturer's Identification Number: A number assigned to each maker of MIDI instruments and used to identify the company when sending a System Exclusive message.

Memory: Special chips used by digital devices to retain information such as patch parameters or digitally recorded sound.

Microprocessor: The chip that is the "brain" of any digital system. It is capable of manipulating and transmitting data as well as performing mathematical operations at great speeds.

MIDI — Musical Instrument Digital Interface: A means by which musical performance and other information is transmitted and received by instruments using a common serial interface. Also the main topic of this book.

MIDI Sync: The mode on a sequencer or drum machine that causes it to start, stop and play at the same tempo as a sequencer or drum machine connected to it.

Millisecond: 1/1000th (.001) of a second.

Mode: In MIDI, the way in which an instrument will respond to incoming MIDI data. The four MIDI modes are *Omni On/Poly, Omni Off/Poly, Omni On/Mono,* and *Omni Off/Mono.* It is possible to command an instrument to change modes via MIDI.

Mode Messages: The MIDI commands used to change the mode of an instrument. These commands tell a MIDI synthesizer to receive data in a certain way.

Modem: A device that allows computers to exchange information over telephone lines. The word is a contraction of "MOdulator/ DEModulator."

Modulation: In synthesis, the periodic changing of a sound's pitch or amplitude. Vibrato is one form of frequency modulation, and tremolo is one form of amplitude modulation. See *"Frequency Modulation"* and *"Amplitude Modulation."*

Modulation Wheel: The controller on a synthesizer used for sending modulation, usually in the form of vibrato.

Monophonic: The performance of a single note at a time.

Mother Keyboard: A term used to describe a keyboard that generates MIDI codes to control other instruments. Often called a *"MIDI controller"* or *"master keyboard."*

MSB — Most Significant Byte: A single data byte that is used to represent the entire numeric range of some parameter.

MTC — MIDI Time Code: A means of synchronizing events between MIDI and SMPTE (video) devices.

Multi-timbral: The capability of some synthesizers to play more than one type of sound or tone color at a time.

Nibble: A half of a byte, or four bits. For example, the lower nibble of a MIDI status byte contains the MIDI channel for the data following.

Note Off: The MIDI code that tells an instrument to stop a note that is currently playing. It consists of three bytes: the status byte (which includes the MIDI channel); the key number (what note it is); and the velocity (how quickly the note is to be released).

Note On: The MIDI code that commands an instrument to play a note. It consists of three bytes: the status byte (which includes the MIDI channel); the key number (what note it is); and the velocity (how fast the key is hit). Note Ons with a velocity of zero are often used to stop a note that is playing.

Omni: A MIDI mode that determines whether an instrument will respond to one or several MIDI channels.

Oscillator: In synthesis, the hardware or software that actually produces sound.

Parameter: A single variable in a group. Parameters in a synthesizer patch would be waveforms, filter settings, or envelope profiles. In MIDI, parameters would include the key number in a Note On event or the position of a pitch bend wheel in a Pitch Bend message.

Patch: The set of parameters for a sound stored in a synthesizer's memory; also called a *"program."* The word "patch" comes from the earlier synthesizers that needed patch chords in order to construct a sound.

Patch Editor: A computer program for creating and modifying patches in an instrument.

Patch Librarian: A computer program used to rearrange and organize the patches within an instrument or instruments.

PC: Personal computer.

Pitch Bend: The act of sliding, or "bending" a note or sound by use of a wheel, slider or knob. MIDI has a code specifically for sending pitch bend messages.

Poly: A MIDI Mode that allows a synthesizer to respond to incoming MIDI messages poly-phonically.

Polyphonic: The performance of more than one note at a time.

Polyphonic Key Pressure: The ability of a keyboard to sense aftertouch on each key individually, and send MIDI messages accordingly.

Port: A device through which computer information is transmitted or received. MIDI uses a port with a five-pin DIN plug.

Portamento: Sliding from one pitch to another. Many synthesizers have this capability as an option. There is a MIDI code for turning this function on and off.

PPQ — Part Per Quarternote: See *"Resolution."*

Program: In synthesis, a set of memory locations within a synthesizer that hold a preset sound. Also called a *"patch."* In computerese, a set of instructions that tells the computer to perform a specific task.

Program Change: The MIDI code that commands an instrument to select one of its patch memories so it can be played.

Quantize: The rounding off of rhythmic values to a particular value such as eighth or sixteenth notes,

usually used to "correct" rhythmic errors. This is used by most sequencers and drum machines.

Release Velocity: The speed with which a key is released. This information is sent with a Note Off message.

Resolution: The number of increments into which a sequencer or drum machine divides a beat. Also referred to as *"timebase"* or *"PPQ"* *(Parts Per Quarternote).*

Reverb: An effects device used to simulate the ambience of a hall or room.

Running Status: A technique used in many MIDI devices to reduce the number of bytes needed to send MIDI messages. This is accomplished by removing redundant status bytes.

Sample: The digital recording of a sound. There are several techniques for digitally recording and reproducing sound. Sampling instruments have the ability to record, store, manipulate, and then play back acoustic sounds. Each key of the keyboard will transpose the sound appropriately to produce a scale.

Sample Dump Standard: A System Exclusive format for MIDI samplers to exchange their memory with other samplers or with computers via MIDI.

Sampler: A digital device capable of sampling. (See *"Sample"*).

Sequencer: In MIDI, a device that records MIDI events, much the way a tape recorder records sounds. Unlike tape recording, however, sequencers record MIDI data, not sound.

Slave: A MIDI device that is controlled by another MIDI device. This can include synthesizers that respond to incoming MIDI information and drum machines or sequencers set to MIDI sync mode.

SMPTE — Society of Motion Picture and Television Engineers: This technical union created the standard synchronization code for film and video.

SMPTE Time Code: A widely used synchronizing code that allows many devices to operate together. It is expressed in hours, minutes, seconds, and frames. See "MTC."

Software: Information in the form of either data or instructions used by a hardware device. A program for a computer. A sample of a sound on a disk. Music on a record or tape. The codes inside the chips in instruments. These are all examples of software.

Song Position Pointer: The MIDI code that instructs a drum machine or sequencer to locate to a specific place in a song for playing.

Song Select: A MIDI code used to to tell sequencers or drum machines which song in their memory to play.

Start: The MIDI code used to tell a sequencer or drum machine to play a song from the beginning.

Status Bytes: The codes that define the *kind* of information being sent in a MIDI message. A status byte is usually followed by one or more data bytes, and also contains the MIDI channel of the event in the lower four bits.

Stop: The MIDI code telling a sequencer or drum machine to stop playing.

Sustain: In MIDI, a controller that causes notes to hold even after Note Off commands have been received.

System Common Messages: The group of MIDI messages used primarily to enhance the functions of other commands. Song Position Pointer, Tune Request, and Song Select are System Common Messages.

System Exclusive Messages: MIDI codes for sending data for a specific instrument. These codes are often used to transfer patch information from one instrument to another, or to program synthesizers remotely through MIDI.

System Real Time Messages: MIDI messages that synchronize sequencers and drum machines. System Real Time messages specify tempo, Start, Stop, Continue and Song Position Pointer.

System Reset: The MIDI command that returns instruments to the condition they were in when first turned on.

Timebase: See *"Resolution."*

Timing Clock: The System Real Time message that is used to synchronize devices. It is sent 24 times per beat.

Tune Request: A MIDI message that commands analog synthesizers to retune their oscillators.

Velocity: In MIDI, the speed with which a key, drum pad, or string is hit or released. This information is sent with all MIDI Note On and Note Off messages.

Velocity Sensitivity: An instrument's ability to detect and respond to velocity. It is not found in all MIDI instruments.

Vibrato: A slight periodic fluctuation of pitch in a sustained note. In technical terms, it is one kind of frequency modulation, typically occurring at rates between about 3 and 7 times per second.

Voltage Control: The technique used by analog synthesizers to represent various patch parameters with voltages.

Volume: The MIDI code used to adjust the overall output level of an instrument. There are 128 possible volume levels (0–127).

Waveform: The shape of a sound depicted graphically as "amplitude over time." Oscillators generate waveforms. Common waveforms in synthesis are sine, square, sawtooth, pulse, and triangle.

For More Information

MIDI is changing, expanding, and adapting to new musical needs almost daily. To stay aware of current events in the world of MIDI, it is well worth your consideration to subscribe to any of the current electronic music periodicals.

The largest MIDI users group is the *International MIDI Association (IMA)*. They provide up-to-date information on MIDI hardware and software through their monthly newsletters. They are also the distributors of the official MIDI Detailed Specification written by the MIDI Manufacturers Association. IMA membership information can be requested by writing to the following address:

International MIDI Association
12439 Magnolia Blvd., Room 104
North Hollywood, California 91607
(818) 505-8964

Some Publications Of Interest

Electronic Musician
5615 W. Cermak Road
Cicero, IL 60650
(312) 762-2193

Keyboard Magazine
Box 2110
Cupertino, CA 95015
(408) 446-1105

The Music Technology Magazine
Music Makers Publications, Inc.
7361 Topanga Canyon Blvd.
Canoga Park, CA 91303
(818) 704-8777

One of the revolutionary aspects of working as an electronic musician today is the ability to communicate with other artists and technicians via computer. With an inexpensive modem, you can be in contact with a large number of people with a vast array of information and skills.

The Performing Artists Network (PAN) is devoted to music and the needs of modern musicians. Services include a bulletin board for communicating with other synthesists, on-line conferences with industry leaders and top musicians, databases with samples and patches that you can load into your own computer, an electronic mail service, a classified ad service, and a variety of other functions geared toward electronic musicians.

PAN Membership costs a one-time sign-up fee of $150, but for buyer's of *"MIDI-The INs, OUTs and THRUs,"* the signup fee is discounted to only $25.00 through June 30, 1988.

ONLINE SIGN-UP PROCEDURES

PAN can be reached by a local call from over 500 U.S. cities and 60 foreign countries, via Uninet or Tymnet. To sign-up, do the following:

1) Dial your local access number. If you have never used Telenet before, call (800) 336-0437 for the number nearest you. Tymnet users can call (800) 336-0149 to find out your local number. You may also dial in directly to (617) 576-0862.

2) When you connect, immediately type your terminal identifier:
Direct: <CR> <CR> (that is: two *RETURNs*)
Telenet: <CR> <CR> (that is: two *RETURNs*)
   When *"TERMINAL="* appears, type: **D1**
   When *"@"* appears, type: **C PAN**
Tymnet: Type the letter **"A"** (without the quotes)
   When *"please login:"* appears, type: **PAN**
Overseas: PAN's international host number is 311061703093

3) In all cases, at *"Username:,"* type: **PANJOIN**

4) At *"Password:,"* type: **RONABOOK**

You will then be welcomed to PAN's On-line Sign-up area, and prompted for all billing information to setup your PAN account.

RATES & CHARGES

PAN Connect-time is billed at $.20 per minute evenings and weekends. Daytime use (7am to 6pm Eastern time, Monday through Friday) is $.40 per minute, except from overseas, which remains at $.20 per minute 'round-the-clock. In all cases, your first minute of connect time is an additional $.25. There is also a $10.00/month mailbox charge*.

There is NO surcharge for 1200 or 2400 baud access.

All charges are billed monthly to your Visa, MasterCard, or American Express.

For further information on PAN, you may write to PAN, P.O. Box 162, Skippack, PA 19474 or call (215) 489-4640.

Prices subject to change.

THANKS...

The author wishes to thank those people who helped me during the writing of this book. I wish first to thank Jim Mothersbaugh, Tadao Sakai and Richard King for showing me this thing called MIDI. Thank you to Thomas Beckmen, president of Roland Corp US, for enrolling me in the greatest MIDI school of all times. Thanks to Chris Meyer of Digidesign for pointing out the occasional folly of my ways, and for understanding all this stuff in the first place. Thanks to Jim Cooper for adding so greatly to my knowledge and to my phone bill.

Thanks go to Ronny Schiff, my editor and agent. If you can understand this, or any other sentence in this book, it is because of her. Thanks to Jaynee Thorne for reading and rereading the materials until it made some sense.

Very special thanks to my friend Scott Wilkinson for the generous looks over both my shoulders, and for the courage to ask the question, "What exactly do you mean here?"

And of course, thanks Mom.

ABOUT THE AUTHOR

Jeff Rona is a composer and arranger of music for film, video, theater and dance, as well as a synthesist, producer, musician, and MIDI software author from Los Angeles. He spent four years as a product developer for Roland, creating computer-based sequencers. He was one of the founders and a past president of the MIDI Manufacturers Association, an international consortium of MIDI hardware and software makers.

ON WRITING & DESIGNING
THIS MIDI BOOK
• TECHNICAL NOTES •

This book was written entirely on an Apple Macintosh. Typesetting commands were inserted on the final draft and the copy was modemed to the typesetter's computer. The typesetter added special font, letter and table spacing commands. Most of the diagrams, chapter heads and page numbers were also designed on the Mac using Full Paint and MacDraw and laser printed.

ABOUT THE COVER...

A digitally synthesized cover for a book about digital synthesizers? Why not?

While musical synthesis has been advancing rapidly, the same thing has been happening in graphic synthesis. A 3-D graphics computer made this cover possible — all the visual elements are synthesized! Here's how:

First the MIDI ring was designed by giving the computer its dimensions. The ring — pins and all — was positioned in "mid-air" by manipulating knobs to move it around.

Next was the creation of the sound waves. Six frequencies' amplitudes were added using a mathematical mixer, and the result was sampled. The sampled values were then fed into something called a "B-spine surface," that filtered the resulting seven-hundred samples into creating tens of thousands of points on a smooth waveform.

One octave of a keyboard was designed by giving the computer the dimensions of a black key, the visible portions of a white key, and how these are ordered to make an octave. Then three octaves of keys were reproduced for the final picture.

Finally, the computer was told that all objects were shiny, and that they were to be placed in a black space. The fill light was dialed down to a deep blue, and the first spotlight was turned on and dialed to yellow. It was moved by knobs until the reflections in the MIDI ring, the sound waves and the keyboard all had proper highlights. The magenta light was turned on and color was placed by the same process. When five *imaginary* spotlights had produced realistic reflections and highlights on all the (non-existent) objects, the setup was saved like a synthesizer patch, and the cover picture was photographed from the computer's screen.

Colin Cantwell is a computer artist, and also has special effects credits in the movies "2001 — A Space Odyssey," "Star Wars" and "War Games." The cover picture was photographed by Colin Cantwell, Crystal Chip Incorporated, using a 4" x 5" transparency.

The editor wishes to thank all of you at Hal Leonard Books and Publishing who form such a kind, cohesive and knowledgeable team, and with whom it is an absolute pleasure to work: Jack Schechinger, who facilitated this project; Glenda Herro, who guided this book through with an infinite amount of patience; Jon Eiche for his eagle eye and recommendations.

And my thanks to Scott Wilkinson...the best friend anyone could wish for.

R.S.